The Story
Newlands Valley

Susan Grant

BOOKCASE

ISBN 1904147178
First Edition 2006
Published by Bookcase, 19 Castle Street, Carlisle, CA3 8SY

Printed and bound by CPI Antony Rowe, Eastbourne

CONTENTS

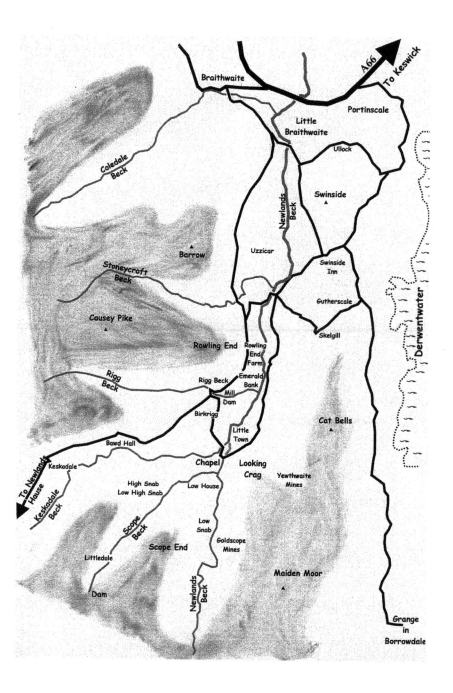

Chapter 1
From Vikings to Manor Courts

"Cat Bells, Maiden Moor, High Spy, Dalehead, Hindscarth, Causey Pike" are names that evoke memories of Lake District holidays for thousands of people. Armies of enthusiastic ramblers have for years and years tramped these exciting peaks, high above the winding beck and smooth green pastures of the valley. It seems an "idyllic" pastoral scene that is seemingly unchanged for centuries.

As long ago as 1778, Thomas West, one of the earliest "tourists", described the Newlands Valley in his Guide to the Lakes as an area of "Alpine Views and Pastoral Scenes in Sublime Style". Some time later, Samuel Taylor Coleridge, poet and friend of Wordsworth, wrote these words in a letter to Sarah Hutchinson: "Newlands is indeed a lovely place, (with) the houses, each in its own little shelter of Ashes and Sycamores, just under the road so that in some places you might leap down on the Roof"; and he admired "the exceeding greenness and pastoral beauty of the Vale itself." Wordsworth

Above: Herdwick in Newlands

Wordsworth's view of Newlands Church

himself was charmed by the vale when he walked the fells with his future wife Mary. Looking down on Newlands Chapel, he wrote:

"How delicate the leafy vale
Through which yon house of God
Gleams midst the peace of this deep dale
By few but Shepherds trod."

Missing, however, from these eloquent but idealised descriptions, is any real awareness of the hard struggle for survival faced by the farmers, labourers and their families. Scraping a living through wind and rain, famine and disease, they cared for their flocks, grew what food they could, made their own clothes, and in many cases proudly carried on the family name for generations. At Keskadale and High Snab, Gillbrow, Birkrigg and Littletown, Skellgill, Uzzicar and Ullock, lived farmers whose names had featured in fifteenth century manorial records. Right through into the twentieth century some of the Fishers, Tickells, Thwaites, Graves and Maysons still lived in the area.

The names of the farms, however, take us back even further to the origins of the earliest settlers. The name "Newlands" came into use only after thirteenth century improvements to the low-lying land between Portinscale and Braithwaite. A system of dykes and drainage channels drew away the water from what had been a swampy impassable marshland, with perhaps a tarn at the lowest point. Before this, the higher land around the formidable range of mountains known as the Derwent Fells, was called Rogersett. Here we have the first clue to the pre-Norman roots of the settlers. Found in early records as Rogersat or Rogersyde, the name is derived from the old Norse, "Roger-saetr". A "saetr" was a summer pasture, often a clearing high in a valley where cattle and sheep could graze in milder weather. Several other Norse names in the area also point to these early Viking herdsmen: Keskadel, the most remote farm in the valley, high up on the road over the Hause to Buttermere, would have been Ketel's "shieling," or "scali". Similarly, Skellgill was the Scale, or Scali, by the ravine. Birk Rigg was built on the Wooded Hillside, High Snab on a rocky bank and Uzzicar, variously recorded as Husekar or Husacre, was " huisa-kjarr", the marsh with the houses. During the years following 800AD, Viking herdsmen searching for new pastures had colonised parts of Ireland and the Isle of Man. It was from there that, in the next century, these Norsemen spread into Cumbria.

For further evidence of the Norse invaders, we only need to look at the "Thwaites" which are scattered around nearby. Thwaite comes from the Norse word "pveit", a clearing in the woods. So we have Braithwaite, ("breoor pveit" or Broad Clearing), Thornthwaite and Stonethwaite, while possibly the oldest of them all is Crosthwaite, the clearing where the cross was set up. Here, legend takes us a long way further back. St. Kentigern was said to have revived Christianity amongst the people of the mountains in 590 AD, choosing as the site of his church, Crosfeld, the small hill north of Keswick. The later name change to Crosthwaite indicates that the Vikings continued to use this clearing as a site for worship.

So, strange as it may seem to us now, it is clear that well over a thousand years ago wandering strangers explored the craggy mountain sides of Newlands, braving the wild animals, the wild weather and possibly the wild natives! In fact, there is little evidence of hostility in this area. The Celtic and Saxon farmers who undoubtedly dwelt around the lake and on the lower slopes above Keswick had probably not penetrated deep into the forests. Close to Newlands, at Ullock, evidence has been found of a Bronze Age burial site, and at Portinscale of a Celtic workshop. But as the Norsemen wandered further from the flat plains of the west coast and the Solway into the land of the Cumri they most likely settled in their summer pastures undisturbed. Bringing with them their own brand of Christianity, they apparently caused no clash of religious practices. In this way, as far as we can tell, began life in the Newlands Valley..

During the eleventh century a major upheaval occurred in the story of the English nation which barely seemed to touch the lives of these Nordic herdsmen and their descendants. In 1066 the unstoppable William of Normandy swept into Southern England with his kinsmen. Very soon he had instigated the survey of his newly conquered lands, which we know as the Domesday Book. But in it we search in vain for any reference to our Cumbrian ancestors. This hostile territory with its craggy mountain passes, rough tracks and lack of welcoming townships was too much of a challenge for the Norman investigators, for whom England ended in Yorkshire. Cumbria was a marginal zone, tossed to and fro between leaders like Owain, King Dunmail, Malcom of Scotland and Earl Gospatrick of Northumberland. William's Norman Lords, however, eventually acquired great tracts of Northern land and in the later years of the eleventh century Ranulph de Meschines was granted the Barony of Allerdale. A motte and bailey type of castle was built for him in Cockermouth, which became the administrative headquarters for Allerdale above Derwent, the area encompassing the fells and valleys around Keswick, Newlands and Bassenthwaite.

During the following three centuries a highly ordered and regulated class system was developing throughout more southern parts of England, with serfs and bondmen, peasants and craftsmen working for the Lord of the Manor. In rural north Cumbria, however, the tenants of the land were largely responsible for their own rough acres, and merely paid rents and fees for their privileges. In the wider river valleys crops were grown, but in an area like Newlands the tending of cattle, sheep and pigs took up the farmer's year. The years of progress in agricultural and social development, under a succession of Norman then Plantagenet Kings, were marred in the Border lands by continued violent disputes between the warrior lords of Scotland and England. Time after time land around Carlisle changed hands. Men were slaughtered, women raped and children abducted. Farmsteads were fortified but still burned to the ground. Happily it seems that the mayhem did not spread south to the families hidden away in Keskadel, Stonycroft, Snabb and their neighbours. The nearest recorded raids took place at Embleton, some eight miles to the north, where out of twenty-four peasant holdings twelve were ransacked and burned.

One aspect of life which was to have a huge influence on many parts of Lakeland, was the setting up of monasteries. Industrious and skilful monks were given land at Furness, Holme Cultram and St. Bees. Alice de Romeli

Stunted sessile oaks clinging to the slopes above Keskadale: remnants of an ancient forest.

who had inherited her estates from the lords of the Barony of Allerdale, sold land in Borrowdale to the monks of Furness Abbey, as well as to the Cistercian monks of Fountains Abbey in Yorkshire. Here they grew corn in the lowlands and raised huge flocks of sheep on the fellsides. To meet the demands of the trade in wool and wood, the monks set up a grange, or store, where the River Derwent flows into Derwentwater and boats could carry the produce across the lake. Thousands of trees were felled, the process we know as the "assarting" of land, to make space, and to be burned for charcoal, while tanneries and bloomeries sprang up in the clearings.

Over the hills the monks did not own the land in Newlands, but the effect of extensive assarting could be seen. High above Keskadale farm we can still see today the remnants of ancient oak forests. Along with those in Borrowdale, these are at the highest altitude of any in England. Stunted and battered, clinging on to steep, stony ground, this is all that remains of a landscape which provided wood for house-building and charcoal burning.

A few miles away from Newlands, Keswick, the little town near the banks of the River Greta, was benefiting from the improvements to local agriculture and trade during the thirteenth century. Oats, barley and corn

9

grown nearby were sold, along with the butter and cheese, which may have given the town its name: Kese(cheese)-wic(town). (Canon H. D. Rawnsley, however, in his book "By Fell and Dale", suggested that in the days of the Norsemen, Ketel, son of Ormr, brought his boats up the Derwent to the lake and landed at "Ketel's Wyke", hence "Kelswick".)

In 1230 Fountains Abbey was given the rights to a fishery in Derwentwater, and in 1276 Keswick was granted a charter to hold a market. The farmers of Rogersett may well have been too poor to have much spare wool to sell in the town. Nor could they well afford to buy any wheat or barley grown on the plains, or clothes and luxuries brought in from distant places. But as later records will show, they continued to set down roots, marrying into neighbouring families and building new dwelling places under the brow of the fells. At Gilbank, High Snab and Low Snab, Skelgill and Gutherscale, several branches of just a few families lived closely together.

Lower down the valley the soggy marshlands of Braithwaite were being reclaimed. Round about 1215 Alice de Romeli granted to Nicholas de Lindford (from the Fountains Abbey area) "land called Pikerig and Fisgardheved in Braithait within these bounds: from Porquenschal ("shelter of the harlots", now Portinscale!) to the stone bridge on the land of Thomas beside the great marsh . . . also the land which was Gilbert the Serjeant's beside the water of Huseker." Boggy land was drained, crops were grown, and it is likely that the little township of Braithwaite was a busy centre of activity by the end of the thirteen hundreds. Professor Angus Winchester, in "The Harvest of the Hills", states that: "Between 1266 and 1310 the rents paid by tenants in the valley rose steadily, reflecting a process of colonisation as peasant farmers extended the cultivated area by gradually enclosing new lands from the waste surrounding their farms."

Roads and tracks were carved through previously unnavigable terrain. Although there was a scant framework of highways dating from Roman times across Cumbria, very few areas of the newly created Crosthwaite Parish were reached easily. Roads from the south, east and west met in Keswick, and the Records of Holme Cultram mention an "ordinary road" through Bassenthwaite. But the state of the tracks winding up to the Rogersett farms must have been a challenge.

Out in the wide world, dramatic events were unfolding. "In the Year of our Lord 1348, about the Feast of the Translation of St. Thomas", wrote a monk of Malmesbury, "the cruel pestilence, terrible to all future ages, came from parts over the sea to the south coast of England, into a port called

Melcombe in Dorsetshire." The pestilence swept across southern England, reaching London in a few weeks, then decimating the population of the entire country. Not quite! We will never know just how aware of the disaster and threat were the Newlands families. Only the remote mountain areas of northern Wales, Cumberland and Northumberland were spared. Whether or not Keswick suffered is unclear. Isolated from the rat-infested towns hit by the plague, it would seem that life in our hill farms may have continued unaffected.

The following century saw England thrown into turmoil as royalty and nobility fought out their claims to the throne in what became known as The Wars of the Roses. The battles between the houses of York and Lancaster took place far away from northern Cumbria, but they had their effect on the lordship of these territories. The Allerdale Estates had fallen under the control of the powerful Percy family of Northumberland in the mid-fourteenth century, when Maud de Lucy married Henry Percy. The Earls of Northumberland were caught up in the fighting throughout the first half of the century, with the second Earl dying in the battle of St. Albans, and the third in the slaughter at Towton in 1461. His lands were forfeited to the crown, but by 1470 his son, another Henry Percy, was re-instated as fourth Earl of Northumberland. It is from this time that we have the earliest written records of life in the Derwent fells. From the proceedings of the local Manor Courts, we learn which of our families lived in each farmstead, who was causing trouble by stealing or neglect of property, and in some cases we meet the ancestors at the distant beginnings of our own family trees.

Chapter 2
Feuding Families and Medieval Law

"At the Court held on the Tuesday next after the Feast of Whitsunday in the 13th. Year of King Edward IV, John Hudson complains of Alexander Fyscher of Newlands in 3 pleas of debt, and that Agnes, late wife of Henry Elyson unlawfully took and kept a child's cradle."

The year is 1474. The place is Cockermouth and the court is hearing the pleas of the tenants of the Derwent fells. Here and there in these Court Rolls we get our first glimpses of day to day life in Newlands. Margaret, "late relict" of John Tykall, complains of Ellen, late wife of John Mayson, in a plea of "trespass", which could mean any misdoing, as in the old Biblical "forgive us our trespasses". (The prefix "late" obviously implied "widowed", not the modern "deceased".) Elsewhere we learn that the wives of John Aldcorn and Robert Piper "are misdoers, for that they pluck the wool from sheep, to wit those of John Stanger and other neighbours". Already we are meeting with family names that will survive in almost the same locations for generations.

As the Wars of the Roses drew to an end in the reign of King Edward IV, life became more settled and the rules and regulations of manorial life controlled the lives of the peasantry. Up in the high Cumbrian valleys

Above: Cattle grazing the meadows near Swinside

however, the pattern of scattered farming communities differed from the class-conscious feudal villages in most of the country. Here, with Landlords far away, many of the farmers were "Customary tenants", paying rent which allowed them virtually to own their properties and pass them on to the next generation. For the small settlements to live productively side by side, a code of acceptable farming practice and responsible tenure of the land had to be followed. Under the carefully regulated legal system of the late fourteen hundreds, the peoples of even these remote Northern areas had their chance to claim justice for unfair practice. Court Rolls were meticulously scribed, at Cockermouth Castle as at other regional centres. Allerdale ward was divided into separate regions including Cockermouth, The Five Towns, and Wigton. The Court of the Derwentfells, meeting sometimes at "Braythuayt", gave verdicts on matters of debt, of stealing, assault and neglect of duties. As we search through the entries, we begin to recognise some of the farming families.

Roll no. 12 Edward IV. The Court of Braythuayt, was held on the morrow of the Feast of the Assumption of the Blessed Virgin Mary in the 13th Year of King Edward IV: it was found by the Inquisition of the jury that Richard Mayson cut and sold wood unlawfully. Several other men were fined for cutting white thorn and mastics in the wood belonging to the King, and it was declared that "John Pele is a wrongdoer for that he taketh by stealth hens and the like. Also he keeps a Black Dog unlawfully". Other matters concerned rents paid to the Lord for the tenants' dwellings: "Robert Fyscher's tenement is damaged and destroyed by water to the amount of 20d a year decrease in value".

The Customary Tenants were, for the most part, the descendants of the old farming families of previous centuries. Because so many of them in the semi-barren upland valley could grow very few crops, and survived mainly through their husbandry of sheep and cattle, their distant landlord, Henry Percy, Fourth Earl of Northumberland, had little interest in their day to day life. A tradition had been established by which the tenant had a right to pass on his property to his own family, the flocks of sheep being part of the settlement. Each 'owner' of property was responsible for its maintenance, as well as that of the hedges and tracks through his land. At each session of the Court, along with 'misdoings' we read of any neglect of such duties.

Roll no.13: the Court of Braythuayt was held on the Wednesday after the Feast of St. Kentigern in the 13th Year of Edward IV, (a rare reference to the Parish of Crosthwaite's Patron Saint). At this sitting detailed accounts of local issues build up a picture of life in 1474 in Newlands: "John Hudson complains of Peter Stele in Rogersett that he shall pay him 17d for wool . . . John Thomson of Scaleshow complains of Thomas Robertson of Newlands that he shall pay him 20d for barley . . . Peter Hudson complains of William Boner of Newlands for trespass . . . Peter Wilkynson complains of Peter Fletcher of Rogerset in two places of debt."

In ensuing sessions of the Court of Braythuayt, between the years 1476-1478, Robert Scott of Newlands was fined for unlawfully owning two cattle, John Fyscher and William Fyscher for fishing in Hussacre Beck and elswhere "at the forbidden season", and others for digging turf where they shouldn't. The very fact that such offences were being considered, does indicate a fairly rigid legal system. One unfortunate individual was fined for allowing a house to get into "a ruinous condition", which was no doubt a nuisance to other families as well as displeasing the landlord. The stealing of sheep and goats was not so much of a problem in Newlands as in other areas. In such inaccessible territory there would be few opportunities for wandering strangers to spirit the animals away.

The name of John Hudson crops up more than once. In 1475 he was complaining again, this time against William Culper, "that he shall pay 16d. for one scythe bought from the plaintiff at Keswyke". It was obviously a bad move to cross swords with John.

At each court sitting, verdicts would be delivered by a jury of twelve or more men representing the area, listed at the beginning of each entry on the Roll. Although at this stage we read just their names, it becomes apparent in later records that there were usually two men from each smaller community involved. Allowing for the fact that so many Christian and family names were duplicated in any one region, it still seems as though on occasion the members of the jury were also the plaintiffs or the accused. The inquisition of the Court in 1476 was carried out by John Mayson, John Croft, Nicholas Bron, John Brondholme, William Fyscher, William Stanger, William Bull, John Bull, John Stub, Thomas Clerk, Peter Tolman, Peter Hudson, John Aldcorn, William Iredale and John Bowes. Men were also appointed to minor positions of authority such as Constables and Viewers of Hedges and Bridges, to ensure that the many regulations of rural life were obeyed. Thus the Viewers of the Hedges in Braythuayt in 1478 "presented" Thomas Williams and his mother for "one defect", and John Mayson of Stonecroft for the same.

Farming was the established way of living in the Newlands Valley in the late fifteenth century. There must have been a certain amount of crop growing, on the lower reclaimed pastures and to a lesser extent in small closes nearer to the upland settlements. The growing of barley and oats, and the movement of livestock, were all subject to strict rules. Sheep, goats and cattle were restricted to certain areas at prescribed seasons of the year. We read that Richard Stub was fined for "pasturing with his oxen at the time of barley sowing", and that Thomas Pele "keepes 30 foreign sheep on the Common". Neighbours were frequently accused of unpaid debts, an indication that real currency was widely in use, not just "goods or kind".

Two family names which have already begun to feature frequently in these records, are the Fyschers and the Maysons. We have already met John Mayson "of Stonecroft" who was fined by the Viewers of hedges in 1478 for "a defect", presumably not keeping his hedges in good order. There is to this day a house in the valley called Stoneycroft. This is perhaps the earliest reference in these manorial documents to a specific dwelling place in Newlands. The will of an earlier John Mayson had been mentioned in 1474, but the next of the family we hear of, a Jacob Mayson in 1501, was just "of Newlands". Here he is, up against the formidable Hudson family again: "It was found by the inquisition that Jacob Mayson of Newlands did riotously and of malice aforethought revile John Hudson of Gayttsgarth saying that the same John had of the goods of him, the said Jacob, for which he has not paid, whereby he unjustly defamed the said John in the full Court of Derwentfells". Jacob was not necessarily at Stonecroft, since, if we jump ahead to 1516, we find the Maysons also living at Husacre, in lower lying land nearby. By the beginning of the sixteenth century a clearer picture develops of families settling and spreading out to other tenements.

The Fyscher family illustrates this development very well. We have already referred several times to the Fyschers in the quoted records, mentioning Alexander, Robert, John and William. They were not necessarily of the same direct family, as we soon learn of Fyschers in other farms. But the earliest recorded home seems to have been Snabb. Today we have farms at High Snab, Low Snab and even Low High Snab, so it is difficult to know exactly which was the original family base. If we again jump to the reign of King Henry VIII, about the year 1516, we find that there is a John Fischer (slight change of spelling) of Snabb amongst the representatives on the Court of Braythuate Jury. By 1520 Robert Fischer and William Fischer were elected Constables for Rogerset.

At the start of the sixteenth century, then, day to day life for the Maysons, Fischers and their neighbours must have centred around the basic necessities of feeding and clothing the family. The wool of the local Herdwick sheep was coarse and greasy, but in these isolated regions the family clothes would be home spun, and garments of black fustion and russet cloth would be tough and hard wearing. The sheep would be heafted as indeed they are to this day. Each flock belonged not to the farm tenant but to the farm itself, so that regardless of changing tenancy the sheep were not moved from place to place. In this way the animals became so accustomed to their own territories that very few would stray, even when loose on the upland fells in the summer. The lambs, once they reached a certain stage, would also be out on the same high rocky slopes, inheriting the same instinct for staying within the boundaries. From the recorded court sessions we know that as well as their cattle and sheep, the farmers could keep perhaps a pig, some goats, hens and a dog, the ownership of these being strictly regulated.

Some of the court cases during the early years of Henry VIII's reign give us an insight into the rules of communal life: "From henceforth no-one shall willingly put any cattle in the moss of Ullak and Braythuate unless it shall be in time of frost, under penalty of 40d." (Roll 14/15 Henry VIII)

Another injunction reminds us that the bracken which has invaded so much of the fellside nowadays, was just as much in evidence then: "It is ordered that no-one from this time forth shall mow the bracken on the hills for burning before the Feast of Michaelmas in any future year under the penalty of 12d. Also that no foreigner (i.e. person not belonging to the township) shall mow or gett covering of twigs for their stakes on the lord's soil without licence under the penalty of 12d for each cartload. Also that anyone who drives sheep or looks after them on the hill from Robertside Moss to Goderscale (Gutherscale near Skelgill) shall visit them once a week between the Feast of the Invention of the Holy Cross and the Feast of St. Michael the Archangel in any future years." (Roll 19 Henry VIII)

Peat played an important role as fuel in those early days, but the digging was strictly controlled: "Also it is ordered that no-one henceforth shall take and carry away any peat fuel in Ullake Moss and Braythuate Moss under penalty of 12d." (Roll 19 Henry VIII)

The practical matters of existence were not all that was controlled by the state. Their souls, too, were supposedly guarded, as in the matter of Sunday Observance: In Roll 25 Henry VIII: "It is ordered that anyone who by himself or his servant shall pass over to any mountain on any festival day or sabbath day before midday shall forfeit to the lord for every such offence (default) unless it shall have been at a time of a great storm or for the saving of any cattle being in danger of death". Presumably the good folk were supposed to be worshipping in church during the Sabbath morning.

Another vital part of existence was the grinding of corn in numerous small mills. With an abundance of water there were many places these cornmills could be set up. By the sixteenth century some of these would already be quite old. Newlands and Braithwaite each had their own. In 1522 it was decreed that, "The mill of Newlands shall no longer from henceforth be kept by any woman but by a sufficient miller under penalty of 6s. 8d." We wonder what goings-on had led to this declaration. In 1525 the corn mill at Braithwaite changed hands after the death of those running it: having been in the hands of John Scott and the wife of William Lees (lady millers still in Braithwaite!) it reverted to the lord of the estate to be demised, with an annual rating value of 13s.3d per year.

Sometimes at a Court of the Derwentfells hearing, the men of "Braythuate" would bring "no presentement". Indeed, it seems that the farming community lived reasonably peaceably together. Away from the seclusion of the valley however, other rural dwellers were not as content. The Rolls numbered 7/8 record that certain men "did gather themselves together at the same time and did rise up in the manner of a new rebellion arrayed in the fashion of war viz. with swords and shields and bows and arrows, bill clubs and steel bonnets and other arms . . . and did enter the lord's liberty of Derwentfells . . . carrying off oats and goods and chattels belonging to Richard Willson of Armathwaite."

Nearer to home, men of Keswick were presented to the inquisition for illegally hunting in the park of John Radcliffe of Derwentwater, Fawe Park, "with bows and arrows and hound and horn, certain wild animals called Fallow deer."

Petty stealing was also frequently recorded, as in the case of "John Lambert of Borodail Grange in the County of Cumberland, Husbandman, on the fourth day of November in the eighth year of King Henry VIII at Newlands in the Liberty of the Derwentfells, one ram of the value of 12d of the goods and chattels of Robert Bell then and there found, did feloniously steal". (From other accounts it seems that the Bell family was at Skelgill, above Stair.)

Punishments other than fines are rarely mentioned but occasionally the clerk of the Court has written in an additional comment. When Margaret, late wife of Robert Dixon, widow, was accused of "unlawfully receiving grain and white and black wool of the goods of Jacob Mirehus at the hands of her sons to the value of 10d", the penalty is also recorded: "Therefore let her be punished with twigs", presumably a beating with a bundle of birches.

Now and then some scandal would spice up the proceedings: "Braythuate presents Margaret Corbett for a scold and harboured by Hugh Atkinson contrary to the penalties", and, "They present the wife of John Hodgeson for taking peat fuel and burning hedges and that she is harboured by Thomas Hodgeson".

These entries taken from the Court Rolls of Henry VIII's reign, have brought us forward into the sixteenth century. This was to be a period of expansion and development in the Valley, with the Crown, the nobility, immigrant workers and new sources of commerce and industry all affecting to some degree the lives of the farmers and labourers.

Chapter 3
The German Invasion

In our study of the Maysons and Fischers of Newlands we have progressed into the early sixteenth century. Far away in London King Henry VIII was consolidating his position of supreme power. Major events of national significance were unfolding. Abroad wars were fought and treaties were signed. We wonder, and doubt, if our farmers and their families heard much about the splendid meeting of King Henry and Francis I of France at the Field of the Cloth of Gold in 1520. How long was it before the Newlands folk heard of the death of Cardinal Wolsey in 1527? Or indeed how much news travelled to Rogersyd of the king's beleaguered and sometimes beheaded wives? No doubt visits to Keswick market would supply them with tales of wonder, and travelling peddlers would bring their own versions of distant events, but with their basic, literally down-to-earth life in the farms, (and no newspaper photographs or television screens to convey dramatic images to their kitchens), they must have had very little idea of what was happening.

Perhaps bonfires were lit on Skiddaw or other high places to celebrate the birth of the Princess Elizabeth in September, 1533, as they were in other

Above: The hidden dam and tiny reservoir high up in Littledale.

Littledale dam, with wall built by German miners.

parts of the country. Rumours of religious upheavals, with Henry proclaiming himself Supreme Head of the Church in England in 1534, and Sir Thomas More dying on the scaffold for his convictions in 1535, may have puzzled and worried many of the people of the mountains and dales.

By 1535 events were taking place which certainly did affect the lives of many people in nearby Borrowdale, as in other parts of Cumbria. Having, for political rather than religious motives, secured his independence from the Church of Rome, Henry turned his attention to the Pope's representatives in England. For many centuries the monasteries had flourished, with the monks cultivating land, becoming astute men of agriculture and trade, and amassing great wealth. With the coffers of England almost running dry through costly foreign exploits, the king viewed these assets with greedy eyes. It was for these riches as much as for fear of opposition that he ordered that the monastic way of life should be dissolved, and assets stripped from the richly furnished Abbeys. Furness Abbey, in the south of Cumberland but with extensive land all over the county, was ransacked in 1537. Fountains Abbey, although way over in Yorkshire, had also held much land in Borrowdale, Keswick, and nearby Portinscale. The monks had established a thriving trade in wool, and had set up barns and storage for grain at Grange in Borrowdale, from where boatloads of produce could be sent by boat over the water to Keswick. When the monks were turned out of their community at Grange the land was sold off to private ownership. The families of Newlands were fortunate in that these massive changes almost on their doorstep did not do much to alter their own tenancy of family holdings. Most of the Valley was in the hands of either the Percy family, Earls of Northumberland, or the crown. Which of these, at

The treacherous slopes of Dalehead, workplace for many German miners.

any given time, depended on relationships between the Percys and the King. Henry Percy the 6th Earl of Northumberland, was weak and ineffective in managing his affairs. Easily led into trouble and debt, he had, by 1531, been obliged to surrender most of his inheritance to the Royal Estates. A royal official at the time is reported to have said, "never have I seen a finer inheritance more blemished by the follies of the owner and untruth of his servants." Life on the farms would scarcely be changed by this, but the tenants would certainly hear of future developments concerning their landlords. Although in an agreement of 1535 Percy received some of his estate back, he was to die two years later, caught up in a dramatic struggle between the king and many of his subjects.

Throughout the 1530s royal decrees had steadily infringed on the traditions and liberties of rural townsfolk and countrymen alike. Taxes rocketed, civic authorities were prevented from carrying out justice, and edicts stated a cancellation of various Saints days and holidays. In the South there had been murmurs of discontent, but in the North things became more heated, with thousands of impoverished labourers hearing rumours that every wedding was going to cost 6s.8d, that they would be taxed for eating white bread, and that the king was going to seize all the ornaments from their churches. Rebellion broke out in Louth in Lincolnshire and very quickly spread through the Northern counties. Led by men of humble origin, the rebels forced landlords to join with them. 30,000 people marched as far as Lincoln in what became known as The Pilgrimage of Grace. There, the Duke of Norfolk was able to dispel the protesters without force, but two years later Henry found an excuse to execute the main leaders and about two hundred helpless peasants. Henry Percy was executed, and, as his two brothers were heavily implicated in The Pilgrimage of Grace, their lands were again confiscated.

It is impossible to think that rumours and eye-witness accounts of all of these troubles, or indeed of the power struggles of the next twenty years, would not have filtered through to the customary tenants of Newlands. But it is safe to say that, based on later evidence of the life of these families, little changed on the farms below Catbells or Causey Pike. This evidence comes to us through two very significant developments in the reign of Queen Elizabeth I. She came to the throne in 1558, and just a few years later the Newlands Valley received attention from the monarch of England in a way it probably has never done since.

In very early times there had been knowledge of rich veins of minerals in the hills near Derwentwater, and there is some evidence of small mining ventures. Several English Kings, from Edward I in the thirteenth century through to Henry VIII in the sixteenth, had granted Charters for the extraction of ores, lead, gold and silver from various sites in the North of England. In the 1400s, Keswick was specifically mentioned as a town "full of miners". For many years, mining activities were carried out by men from Bavaria, Holland and Germany, countries where technical and managerial skills had developed far beyond those of English workers.

The first few years of Elizabeth's reign saw a burgeoning of industry and trade, giving rise to renewed interest in such a valuable commodity. In 1561 the Queen granted an indenture to Mr. Thomas Thurland, rector of Gamston in Nottingham, and the German, Johann Steinburger, for investigating the possibility of a mining venture in the North of England. Three years later the grants were transferred to Thurland and a Daniel Hechstetter, an agent for a wealthy firm in Augsburg. These two were to search for "All manner of mines and ures of gold, silver, copper and quicksilver" in many counties of England. I have quoted from "Elizabethan Keswick" written by W.G. Collingwood. In 1912 Collingwood was able to study the original accounts from Augsburg of the mining activities in the Keswick area from

Wheelshaft deep in the Goldscope mine.

1564 to 1577. Aspects of these activities has been well covered by several writers, who have drawn on these and other documents. The most recent account is Ian Tyler's practical and detailed study, "Goldscope and the Mines of the Derwent Fells" (Blue Rock Publications 2005). Here, however, we will look at not so much at the technical features or financial problems of the newly formed "Company of the Mines Royal", but the extent to which any of the Newlands farming families became involved with the Germans.

For a few years the Newlands mines became the most productive in the area. Shafts were driven into the ancient rocks above the farms at Stoneycroft, Littletown, Snab and further up the valley at Dalehead. Even now, some 450 years later, a walk up the hidden valley of Littledale reveals the small dam creating a reservoir, high above Low House farm, to supply a controlled but somewhat unreliable water supply.

During that period the bulk of the workforce was made up not of Englishmen, but of German miners brought over especially to work for the new Company. An extract from the Records of the Privy Council is quoted by Collingwood: "At Grenewich the viijth of July 1565. A letter to the mayour and other officers of Newcastle that there be presently certaine Almaynes, to the nomber of xl or l, looked for to arryve at that town within theese x dayes, they are willed to cause the sayd Almaynes to be for theyr monny curtesly receyved and used, and by theyr good order guyded and conducted from Newcastle to Keswyk in Cumberlande, the place where they are appoynted to rest and woorke."

We wonder what these visitors thought of their new home town. By all accounts, Keswick was at that time a very small, muddy market town, with only two inns, (one of which housed Daniel Hechstetter when he arrived to supervise the mining), several ale-houses, rough and ready stone-built cottages and little sanitation. Many of the miners found accommodation here, but others were lodged in Braithwaite and some in the Newlands farms. As time passed, the stones of the valley would also be used to build rough and ready barrack-like dwellings for short spells of occupancy, to spare the miners at the top end of Newlands, under the shadow of Dalehead and High Spy, the long trek back to civilisation every day. And so the Fischers, Maisons, Bonners and Scotts of Newlands, became accustomed to seeing columns of foreigners tramping along the valley and hillside tracks at the start of their day's work, and hearing the clanking, banging and thudding of men and machinery high on the fellsides above their farms.

In 1566 hostilities broke out between the Queen and Thomas Percy, Seventh Earl of Northumberland. Percy was not included among the many shareholders of the mining company, but, realising that riches were to be found on his land, sent men to stop the Germans from removing ore. But before his objection, a reported 600,000lbs of ore had been raised at the "Gottes Gab" (God's Gift) shaft near Low Snab, later known as Goldscope. A long and complicated legal battle resulted in a decision in 1568 by the judges and barons of the Exchequer that, "as there was more gold and silver in these mines than copper and lead, (doubtful) the Queen was within her rights in reclaiming them." (Elizabethan Keswick p. 25)

Again, the inhabitants of the valley must have been aware of the disturbances and arguments on the hillsides around them. Other events outside the area were momentous enough, but had little relevance to the new industrial ventures around Keswick. In May, 1568, Queen Elizabeth had a potentially dangerous situation to resolve, with the arrival of Mary Queen of Scots by boat at Workington. England was under the rule of the Protestant Elizabeth, and many Catholics holding true to the supremacy of Rome were ready to support Mary's claim to the English throne. But Elizabeth was more than a match for her would-be rival. Mary was escorted to Cockermouth, not so many miles from the mining activies near Keswick. There, the partly ruined

Spoilheaps at the entrance to the Goldscope mine.

castle was declared unfit for her habitation and she found board in Cockermouth Hall, the home of Henry Fletcher who was heavily involved with the Germans. From there she travelled to Carlisle, where the Earl of Northumberland demanded custody of her. This was refused, causing yet another rift between Thomas Percy and his Queen. In the following year the doomed Percy of Northumberland was imprisoned in Scotland after leading the failed Rising of the North. He was finally executed in 1572, yet another Percy to fall foul of an English monarch.

Against this background of faction and intrigue, the new arrivals in the North West and their local hosts continued with daily business. Turning now to a detailed study of the transactions in Collingwoods accounts, we can trace various ways in which the farmers and labourers supplemented their meagre incomes with payments for services rendered to the miners.

Collingwood's study of the Augsburg accounts for the years 1564 to 1568 gives information relating to diplomacy, correspondence and finances, but little of local interest. However, in 1569 the first of the Keswick Journals appears, and it is in this and the subsequent journals up to 1577 that such names as Skot, Ryg, Maison, Bonner, Fischer and others appear. Many families in the area did, of course, share the same surname, so it is not always possible to be sure of their dwelling places.

In a list of men sorting the ore at "God' Gift", we find:-Adam Wyllemson; Harry Fischer; John Dawson; Edi Alleson; Adam Pirson (Pearson); Toby Norman; John Bell; James Dickheson; John Ponner(Bonner); John Fletscher; John Bue(Bowe); Thomas Hundter; Meils(Miles) Watson; Thomas Fyscher; Niclaus Dickheson (all at 5d a day.)

Other men did more constructive work: John Scot and others were paid 18d for 14 "skep" of lime, and carriage at 32d totalling £5.4s.3d. John Grave, a messenger, was given a year's wages of £3. English day-labourers for carriage of wood on time-work did 190 shifts at 2d. a time. For emptying the water-shaft at God's Gift 6/8d was paid out. John Bull, as foreman of the Englishmen at Newlands for two terms received 5/-. Local skills came in useful: John Fischer, for building a dry wall at the water courses and weir, was paid for twelve days at 12d. and for 18 days at 9d.

The 1569 Whitsuntide reckonings showed that at the Newlands Stampworks English labourers dug foundations of watercourses and carpenters spent 91 days at 10d. a day cutting two axels for water wheels, a "Senstock", big posts, and other timber. £26.13s 8d was paid out to labourers carrying wood, scrap iron etc. and for breaking up a big stone in the road to Newlands. John Fischer the waller was busy again, being paid £8 for his work, while John Sanderson cut 70 sods for 18/6 and a rod plank for 11/6.

Not all expenses paid to Englishmen were for labour. An entry for June states that John Bonner of Newlands received 2/4d for a stable "where our horses rest at midday, this summer till Maria Magdalena." (July 22). Horses' food at Newlands, for 2/10d, also featured in the accounts. Care of horses would often be needed from local people, as would some degree of hospitality. Although most of the immigrants were housed in Keswick, there are records of rents paid out in Newlands. "Christl Clarickh's (Clark's) widow at Newlands, for the room in which the watchman lies and keeps all his iron and tallow, to Jan. 1st, 10/-." followed by, "Hue Fischer, at Newlands, house in which single men live, to Oct. 16, 17/6d." The standard of accommodation may not always have been up to the German Overseers' liking, as an earlier entry records: "The house where we eat needed 15 ells of coarse canvas over the dining room to keep bats out."

In 1709, a survey of the old mines was published by Thomas Robinson, who had himself tried to re-work some Newlands mines. The skill of the German miners was reflected in his findings: "Of all which veins the richest was that they called Gowd-Scalp. We found the vein wrought three yards wide and twenty fathoms deep above the grand level, which is driven in a hard rock a hundred fathom, and only with pick-axe, hammer and wedge, the art of blasting with gunpowder being not then discovered. For securing of this rich vein, no cost of the best oak-wood was spared; and for the recovering of the soles under the level was placed a water gin, and water was brought to it in troughs of wood on the tops of high mountains, near half-a-mile from the vein".

As well as the shafts at God's Gift, the names of several other mines in the German accounts relate to Newlands. Thus at the "Bagpipes" John Studdart was working, while Thomas Judall(Youdall) and Robert Mayson were at the "St. Joseph". At the New Cut "below Littleton" were 3 other men, with D. Fyscher and D. Faschet sweeping in the Nick below Littleton. A very significant list of names is given towards the end of 1569 in relation to the carriage of Ore. Some of these men we will meet later!

Robert Mayson, carried 300 kibbles from God's Gift to the water in the Vorwald (Copperheap Bay on Derwentwater?). Wyllem Fyscher Gilbanckh, Richard Tyckhell, Thomas Haynes, John Fyscher Gilbanckh, Margareth Klearckh, John Bowe and others, various quantities to the lakeside or Newlands stamp. Also at the Newlands stamp, drinks to the value of 1/6d were offered to the Newlands farmers who helped to carry the wheel axle.

It is perhaps too easy, in our present age of global travel, familiarity with foreign languages and awareness of different cultures, to underestimate the impact of this German invasion. It is unlikely that many of the "dutchmen" spoke English, and highly improbable that Newlands farmers spoke German! The gruelling, claustrophobic work of tunnelling out the mine shafts was a world away from the open-air, weather-buffeted life-style of the farming families. Tensions must have arisen from time to time between employers and workmen, miners and farmers, and even husbands and wives as they adapted to new ways of life. There are stories of hostility and violence against the Germans in Keswick, but on close inspection the records show very little evidence. The visitors in fact found a very convenient and practical way of keeping out of troublesome situations. They bought Vicar's Island in Derwentwater and set up a community, building a windmill, brewery, pigstyes, pigeon house and garden.

Back in Newlands, by 1571, Dick Walker, George Fischer and Nicholas Fischer were foremen at God's Gift. That year saw a serious accident at the crusher in Newlands, with Robert Banke receiving injuries for which he was treated by the German surgeon Israel Waltz. The risk of accident was extremely high, but it seems, amazingly, that not very many lives were lost. In 1573 "certain farmers who found new mines" were paid 3/-, and later we read, "given to a farmer, Cristoffer Boner, for finding the mine at St. Reichart, 2/6d. Many of the others previously named were also still employed from time to time, amongst them Davitt Bell (David Bell), John Boner, Margaret Clerckha, Hugh Vischer, John Fischer "of de Schnapes" (ie: Snabs) and John Fischer of "Low Schnap". We are beginning to read more detailed information about the exact dwellings of these men. In a 1574 list of creditors to the German Mines we find: Willum Studert of Littleton, Wullum Studert of Stainekrafft (Stoneycroft) and Wilum Thowson of Kesskadel. We can now build up a picture of where these families lived.

However, by this time, another far more significant aspect of record-keeping had started. From the year 1562, Registers of Births, Marriages and Deaths were kept in Crosthwaite Parish Church. It is therefore possible to link the families we have been following and discover who was related to whom! And as a footnote to accounts of the German visitors, we can trace which if any of the many "mixed marriages" in the Crosthwaite records involved local lasses.

The first recorded entries of Germans marrying locally were of Hans Haring, foreman at the Newlands mine, and Isabella Atkinson, in September 1565, then Simon Pusbargar, "theutonicus", to Janet Fischer of Grange in Borrowdale, in the November. Here there is also a Newlands connection: a generation later, in January 1597 a Susan Puphbarger of Stoneycroft, infant, was buried at Crosthwaite, and a Symon Puphbarger "of Stare" later that year. In 1599 a John Puphbarger, possibly another son, married Jennet Fisher of Newlands.

On November 23rd, 1567, Hans Moser, "Duchman", married Elizabeth Clarke of Newlands. (Almost all of the Crosthwaite records call the Germans Duchmen.) That he remained in the Valley is born out by entries of the births of several children between 1567 and 1578. Eventually Hans Moser of Newlands died in 1593. Perhaps the most significant marriage was the second one of Hans Haring ("Herring" in the registers). His first wife, Isabella, had died in 1574, leaving him with daughters Janet, Barbara, Frances and Annamaria. He married Janet Studdert of Rogersyde on 29th May, 1575. In the Keswick journals we read that he was given a gift of 15/- on this occasion. A few paragraphs later we learn that £1 was paid to "H. Hering's daughter in London". Janet Studdert then continued the Haring dynasty by producing a son, Thomas, as well as several daughters.

Between 1565 and 1584 parish records show the births of 176 children to the German miners. It is in the following generation, therefore, that we see further evidence that they were accepted by Newlands families: "30th August 1590: William Slegell, Duchman, m. Agnes Peele of Newlands. . . . 27th September 1590: Xpofer (Christopher) Clocker of Newlands m. Alice Stanger of Skelgell. . . . 11th November 1594: Bartholomew Woulfe, Duchman, m. Janet Bonner of Newlands."

However, returning to the Parish Registers of the 1560s and 70s, and leaving the realm of mixed-nationality marriages, some detective work brings us to the conclusion that the Fisher family dominated the hillsides and were probably responsible for the original building of several farmsteads. Between the first time we met a Fyscher, (Alexander in 1474), and the start of the Registers, there is a gap of three or four generations. The burial of a Margaret Fyscher of Snabb, "wedow", in 1566, establishes the continuation of the name. We do not know who had been her husband, but the reference to her home as Snabb links her to the fifteenth century family. The earlier record of Robertus Fischer marrying Margaret Atkynson in 1563 begins the entries for the next generation. An Elizabeth Fischer married John Peale of Rogersyd in 1567, and in October of that year the marriage was celebrated between Hugh Fysher and Elizabeth Hudson. Hugh seems to have inherited the family farm, as Snabb was listed as the birthplace of his children: Katherine in 1570, Esaybel in 1572, Margaret who died in infancy, John in 1574 and Elizabeth in 1597. However, to add to the complications, the marriage of another Hugh Fischer also took place, a month later, in 1567. The entry reads: "Nov. 30th Hugh Fysher of Newlands m. Elizabeth Dickson, single woman". The term "single woman" in these records meant a woman who has had a child whilst unmarried. The question of where this second Hugh Fisher lived is probably answered for us by some of the details in the Keswick mining journals. In a list of 1574 we find amongst the creditors to the mines, " Heuge Fischer wife of Neulandt" and, "Heuge Fisher in Neulandt in the Lowschnap" i.e.:Low Snab. Perhaps this was the "Hue Fischer" who received payment for housing "single men" in 1577. Low Snab is a farmstead on the slopes of Scope End, below what is now "High Snab". Hugh was not alone in Low Snab. Also recorded there is a John Fischer, who was still carrying loads of peat for the mines in 1577.

To return to the Births, Marriages and Deaths. A few months after the burial of Margaret Fyscher in 1566 comes that of "Margaret Fysher of Gilbancke, wedow". Yet another farm is added to the Fyscher dynasty.

Gilbank is on the eastern side of the Valley, not far from Littletown. An Agnes Fyscher of Gilbancke is buried in March, 1572, and an Esabell in the April of the following year. The Gibancke Fyschers were not having a good time. But the line continued, and in 1574 the baptisms included Richard, son of Richard Fysher of Gilbank and Janet. Then, in 1576, John Fysher of Gilbank married Margaret Hodgehon of Portinscale. If it is confusing for us to sort out the Fysher families, it must have been even more so for the Germans. But identification was made easier by the fact that double-barrelled names began to appear in their accounts. Thus we have Wyllem Fyscher-Gilbanckh and John Fyscher-Gilbanckh in 1569, and by 1571 the two names appear in that form again with a note in parenthesis reading "Fyscher-Gilbanckh (always thus)".

Just as we think we have untangled the web of Fyschers we notice another baptismal entry in 1566 reading, "Nov.1st Robert, son of Robert Fysher of Newlands and Esaybell". Where in Newlands? We soon find out: "May 1568, Margaret, daughter of Robert Fysher of Birekrigg and Esaybell". Introducing Birkrigg, still a family home high above the Valley floor. While Robert and Esaybell were adding to their family almost every alternate year, along comes, "John, son of Xpofer Fysher of Birkrig and Janet" in 1577. (In 1574 and 1575 burials had taken place of a Magdalene then a Gawine Fysher of Byrkrigge.) I think that we can now confidently assert that the upper Newlands valley in the later sixteenth century "belonged" the Fysher family. (There were still others, but we don't need to mention them all.)

As we have seen, the arrival of The Company of The Mines Royal in this remote Lake District valley must have meant great changes in many lives. But there were other families less involved in the mining, whose lives continued more or less unchanged. It is time now to look more closely at the lands and very basic possessions of some of these.

Chapter 4
Surveys and Suffering

In 1578, some twelve years after the arrival of the German miners in Newlands, a major survey was carried out for Henry Percy the eighth Earl of Northumberland. Later to earn a reputation as "Cruel Henry", he had succeeded to the title after the execution of his brother. Only too aware of the hostilities and tensions between the Percy family and Queen Elizabeth, he wanted detailed knowledge of all the estates he had inherited in the Northern counties. Fortunately for our study of Newlands, these included all the tenant-held farms in the higher reaches of the valley as well as in Braithwaite and Thornthwaite villages. The commissioners listed over thirty tenements or "parcels" of land, giving the names of the "customary tenants", the rents paid, and detailed accounts of dwellings, barns and outhouses. So, we can now sort out just who lived where. With only a few exceptions, each farmholding listed in the survey is still identifiable today, almost four hundred and thirty years later!

We have already paid a lot of attention to the Fischers and the

Above: Low House Farm, hidden among the trees today. Could this be the site of Undertown in the Percy Survey?

Maysons, so let's leave them aside for the moment and meet the other families living far up the Valley, below the fells.

At Littletown a Christopher Clerke paid 8s.8d. rent for a tenement house, two barns and a chamber house. Around the buildings were his small plots of land: arable, pasture and meadow. The details of these are typical of all the small farms. "A close of arable adjoining called the Well Parrock containing one acre and a half. One close of arable pasture and goode ground called High Close containing 6 acres. A parcel of arable and meadow called Gill Acre containing one acre and a half. One close of arable meadow and goode ground called Cote Acre containing 2 acres. A parcel of meadow called The Nether Side of the field containing 3 roods with sufficient common of pasture." That last item referred to Christopher's right to graze his sheep on the "Common Land", but the numbers of his animals would be within certain limits. The Clerkes had occasionally featured in previous Rogersett records. Amongst the court jurors of 1476 was a Thomas Clerk, and almost a hundred years later, in the accounts of the German miners, we have already met "Christel Clarick's widow" and a Margaret Clerckha, possibly the same lady who provided a room for the night watchman. In October 1571 the family made an ignominious entrance into the Crosthwaite parish records with a baptism of "Elizabeth, daughter of John Clarke of Newlands, single man, and Esaybell Yowdall of the Same, wedow, Basse gotten." By 1575, however, their relationship seems to have been legitimised, with the record of the baptism of "John, son of John Clarke of Snabb and Esaybell". Probably John was a relation, possibly brother, of Christopher. By 1578 both John and another Clerke, James, were among the tenants at the Snabb farms. In 1577, the year before the survey, the parish registers show that a daughter Elizabeth was born to Xpofer Clarke of Lyteldell and Janet. (For many years the form of the name with the X was used in records.) Littledale is now just the name of the very isolated, almost hidden valley under the eastern slopes of Robinson. Two years later we read of the baptism of John, son of Xpofer Clarke and Janet of Lityldall. The use of this name as their dwelling place is a bit of a mystery: from subsequent records we find that "Littledale" usually refers to Low Snab farm, so it seems clear that around this time, the Clark family were expanding and moving around different neighbouring properties.

To return to the Percy Survey entry on Christopher Clerke's lands at Littletown: an interesting postscript reminds us of the presence of the German miners: "The Well Parrock aforesaid, and divers other places of the said tenement, is clean wasted and burnt with the water that descendeth from the

Ure gotten by the Duchmen."

Time now to look at a name which occurs only once in the Percy Survey: "Christopher Peale (from the surrender of John his father) holdeth two tenement houses and other buildings, a garth containing one quarter of a roode, three closes of arable and meadow adjoining called Undertown". Hopefully the Peales had mended their ways since the days when, in 1474, Thomas Pele kept 30 "foreign" sheep on the common and John Pele, the wrongdoer, "did take by stealth hens and the like!" By 1516 a Richard Peil of Gilbank was a juror. Obviously the Peeles, like so many others, moved around from farm to farm. "Janeta Peyll filia Ricardi" was baptised in 1562, followed by "Guillemus Peyll filius Xpofer" in 1565. Then John Peyll of Rogersyd and his wife Elizabeth produced daughter Janet in 1568 and son Xpofer in 1571.

The location of Christopher Peale's tenement at "Undertown" is something of a mystery. Two other survey entries name this as the position of tenement houses, barns and other buildings. We find Nicholas Fischer of Undertown, (in right of his wife), paying 6s.10d. and John Studdart of the same giving 6s.6d, both small amounts. Together with Christopher Peale's houses, they must have formed quite a sizeable community. These entries come early in the section of the Survey headed Rogersett, indicating a situation higher rather than lower in the vale. All the names in this area, the Peeles, Studdarts, Robinsons and Bonners, when referred to in Parish records, are just listed as "Rogersyde". In the Survey, these same farmers are listed as tenants of houses with such names as "Thwate", "Riddings", "Cote" and "Rigg Close", all grouped together near Undertown. Could Undertown have been the area around what is now "Low House", in an area of arable land near the Chapel, as this name is significantly absent in the Survey?

To return to Christopher Peele, we learn that his lands included a parcel of arable called Acre containing one roode and a half, one close of arable and pasture called Holme Ridding containing one acre two roodes, and several other similar small parcels or closes for which he paid a total of 8s.7d rent. For the remaining years of the sixteenth century the Peeles, (with the customary variation in spelling), continued to marry into other old Newlands families.

Another well-established family mentioned in the Survey are the Scotts at Birkrigg. They featured in The Manor Court Rolls of the previous century, when Robert Scott of Newlands fined by the Court of the Derwent Fells for unlawfully owning "two cattle", and both John and Christopher Scott

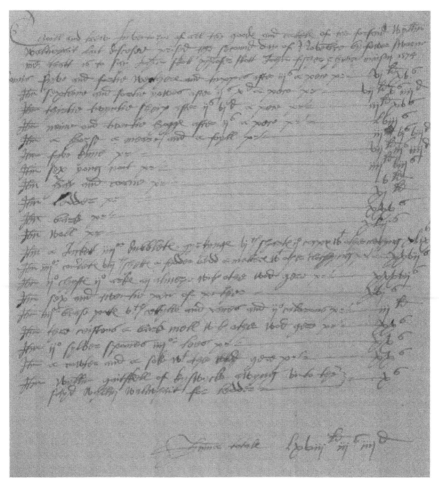

Inventory of William Walkthwaite, a sixteenth century Farmer and Tanner.

were witnesses to the will of their neighbour Wliiam Walkthwaite in 1574. The Survey gives us John Scott the Younger with his tenement house, little garth, acres of arable land and pasture. Among his lands, for which he paid a total of 6s.5d. in rent, is a meadow intriguingly named "Fish Shuttle", presumably down by the beck. John Scott the Elder also held a tenement at Birk Rigg, with a barn, a "little sheep house", various parcels of land, and a share also in the Fish Shuttle.

In the study of these early farming settlements, it has become very apparent that the men and women alike rarely moved far out of the valley to find eligible marriage partners. Indeed, it is often difficult to sort out the proliferation of similar names! However, in the 1578 records one brand new name does appear. Survey entry no. 17 states that one of the Snabb tenements is held by William Dover, "in right of his wife". We have come across this phrase already, in quoting the Nicholas Fischer tenement at Undertown. In such cases, the lady in question has inherited a farm, and when she has married, her new husband has moved in as farmer and rent-payer. In the case of Nicholas, the marriage of a man of his name and an Essaybell Thwait may be the key. But with the arrival of William Dover at Snabb, a whole new dynasty was begun. William is recorded in the Parish registers, when he married into the Fischer family, as coming from a prosperous and widely scattered farming family in the Bassenthwaite area. From a distance of at least six miles, here was a real foreigner! There are early references to connections between these two dominant families in their regions. The mystery of the story behind the marriage deepens when we look at the details of the marriage entry:

"1574: William Dover of Bassenthwaite and Elizabeth Fischer (alias Dickson) of Newlands." Alias, in these registers, usually referred to a previous change of surname, for one of several possible reasons, but without any disreputable connotations. So, who was this Elizabeth, and why the multiple names? More detective work soon solves this particular puzzle. In chapter 3 we discovered that two Hugh Fischers had married girls called Elizabeth in 1567: the first, an Elizabeth Hudson who after her marriage in the October went on to produce sons and daughters at Snabb throughout the next fifteen years. But the other Hugh had married Elizabeth Dickson, a "singlewoman". This term indicated that the young lady had previously borne a child out of wedlock. With two lovers already accounted for, the excitement in Elizabeth's life was far from over. It seems that in 1573 Hugh Fischer died, leaving his widow, nee Dickson, free to marry William Dover! At last her life seems to have settled down, as she and William soon produced a young Will and continued with Robert, Elizabeth, Thomas and Richard.

A last look at a Survey family will lead us on to a picture of daily life in the farms in the 1700s. At entry no. 5 is William Walkthwat, with a tenement house and a barn somewhere in Rogersett. At nos. 26 and 31, John Thwate the Elder and John Thwate the Younger hold tenements at Keskadell. The Parish registers in previous years had clearly stated that those living in "Keskaydell", marrying and producing children, were Walkthuats or

Walthuats. Yet at the same time the records of their births and marriages seemed to mix the names at random. A hundred years earlier, in the 1477 court rolls, Christopher and James Walkthuayt were called to account for debt, but on the whole they seemed to keep themselves out of trouble. In the eighth year of Henry VIII, 1516, the jury included William Walkthuate of Rogersett and in 1519 he was joined by John Walkthuate of Keskendell. By the time of the Survey we can be quite sure that the same family was represented at this farmholding, the highest and most remote in Newlands.

Four years before the Survey, in 1574, the burial had taken place of "William Walkthuayt of Keskendall." In the records office in Carlisle we can read a copy of his will! What is even more fascinating for our story is the copy also of the inventory of his possessions. Here is an amazing chance to learn a little more about the lives of our 16th century farmers. At the beginning of his last will and testament, written on the third day of October anno domini 1574, William, "fearing the pangs of death yet whole of mind and in perfect remembrance, (praise be to God)," follows the customary proceedings of commending his soul to Almighty God, trusting in the Passion of our Saviour Jesus Christ to be one of the elect children of God, and giving his body to be buried in the churchyard of Crosthwaite. He then outlines his wishes for his family. He gives to John, his son, the title and rights to his farmhold. Here we witness the long-established custom of the tenants-at-will to pass on their property to the eldest son, even though they are still paying rent to the Earl of Northumberland to live there. John is to give five pounds to William's youngest son Hugh, (born 1567), and Janet, his widow is to be allowed to continue to live in the house. His youngest daughter, Agnes, (later to marry William Dover junior) is given a sum of money linked to "goodes and beddying", possibly serving as a dowry. The residue of all his goods and chattels, after funeral expenses, goes to Janett his wife, and Jannet, Esaybell and Margareth, his elder daughters, who are also executors of the will.

Evidently we are reading of a large, close-knit family, following a well-established custom of handing down property and possessions. In the Inventory that follows, we get an insight into the Walkthwaites' way of life. According to custom, William's goods and chattels were evaluated by "four sworn men", usually reliable neighbours. So, for William, we have John Scott, Christopher Scott, John Fisher and Henry Maison. We have met them all before.

The first items listed in inventories were always the livestock, the most important of the farmers' possessions.

"Imprimis: fyve and fortie weythers .." - here we are introduced to the age-old dialect names for Cumbrian sheep, still used in the twentieth century, a "wether" being a male sheep.

"Item: Sexteine and fortie yewes

Item: Thirtie twyntie sheip. "

After the sheep come "Neine and twentie hogges", not pigs, but one year- old lambs.

Other animals are a horse, a mare and a foal, and five cows. These are followed by a quantity of hay and corn. Other farms further down the valley where land was more fertile, would produce oats as well, but these are not mentioned here. What is of more interest is the recording of William's stocks of wood, "wood-gere", bark and leather, a bark mell and other bits of gear which point to an active involvment in the craft of tanning.

As we have noted earlier, some of the oldest remaining native woodland in the county is to be found on the slopes high above this farm. In the 16th century many more trees would still be growing on the mountains, above the intake areas for sheep. On a small scale the tanning business carried on in the valley would add to the wealth of the farmers, as well as providing a source for their own families' clothing. At the end of the inventory is the statement that William was owed money for leather by Wylliam Gaitskell of "Kyswycke." Also in the Inventory we learn that the Walkthwaites' possessed six and thirty pieces of pewter, brass pots, cauldrons, and even two silver spoons. Add to that, the value of his clothing, his feather bed and mattress, and the total assets amount not to a fortune, but to enough to keep the family together.

The Walkthwaites were not the wealthiest of the Newlands families, but we can see how their life fits generally into the pattern of upland farming at the time. To give a wider view, we find reports such as that in a 1570 summary for the crown, of the lands in the Honor of Cockermouth belonging to the attainted 7th Earl of Northumberland:

"Albeyt the Countrey consyst most in wast grounds and ys very cold, hard and barren for the wynter, yet ys yt very populous and bredyth tall men and hard of nature, whose habitaciouns are most in the valleys and dales where every man hath a small porcion of ground; which, albeyt the soyle be hard of nature, yet by continuall travell ys made fertyle to there great releyf and comfort for there greatest gaine consysts in breeding of cattle which are no charge to them in the Somer by reason they are pastured and fedd upon the mountaines and waste . . . They have but little tillage, by reason whereof they lyve hardly and at ease, which mayth them tall of personage and hable to endure hardness when necessyte requyryth."

This report is quoted by Angus Winchester in "Harvest of the Hills", (Edinburgh University Press 2000), and also by Andrew Appleby in "Famine in Tudor and Stuart England" (Liverpool University Press, 1978). From these and other studies we can build a picture of the hand to mouth existence of rural communities in Cumberland and Westmorland. Appleby describes the typical living of an upland farmer in the Crosthwaite area : "The farmer grew what corn he could on his limited arable and relied on the seemingly endless pasture to maintain his livestock. And he hoped that the proceeds from the sale of his animals or their hides, wool, woolfells (or woolskins), tallow and meat would enable him to buy grain if his own arable holding did produce enough to feed his family".

From other probate inventories we learn of their dependency on sales of wool, hides, and tallow for candles, on the cultivation of oats, and the rougher variety "bigge", rather than wheat, which would be grown in more fertile valleys.

1596 saw the death of John Thwaite, son of William, of Keskadell. We have both his will and the "whoole, trew and prfect Inventorie of all the goods and chatles moveable and unmoveable as were John Thwaites of Keskadell senior at the day of his death, prysed by foure swoorne men, viz, William Towson, John Scott senior, Christopher Fisher and John Mayson."

The Inventory reveals the typical possessions of a Newlands farmer:

Imprimis: 40 old sheep and 4 hogs	£6-13-4d
2 kyne and a half. 2 hefferes. 1 stagge (horse)	£5-13-4d
pleugh and plew geare, spaids and other Implements	£0-10-0d
coorne and heye	£4- 6-8d
caldren with fyre vessell and peuther dublers	£0-17-0d
wooden vessell. 1 wheel and 1 crooke	£0- 9-0d
his apparrell	£0-18-0d
1 covercloth with rest of all beddinge. 1 winding cloth	£0-23-4d
2 sackes	£0- 2-8d
1 cheest, 1 almery, 1 arke	£0-23-4d
flesh	£0-0-20d
1 sadle, bridle and gyrder	£0-0-18d
wolm clooke	£0-10-0d

The most interesting aspect of this inventory, however, reflects what seems to have been a general state of affairs among the farming community - a relaxed approach to lending and borrowing money. Perhaps John was called to meet his maker suddenly, before he had sorted his financial affairs, for this list of his goods is followed by an extremely lengthy account of the debts he owed to others. His son William and several of his neighbours were waiting for payments for goods or services rendered. His son-in-law, John Coudall, must have bailed him out frequently, as not only was he owed £14-0-0d, but also money for a meal "which was borrowed", and sum of 33s.4d for "certain geare". Two amounts were due to the Chappell of Newlands, possibly the "statutory" fees, while Isabell Thwaite senior was awaiting payment for some woole. Ladies, in fact, feature very largely among John Thwaites' creditors. Perhaps he had charmed the wives of John Mayson, Robert Mayson, William Dover, William Murrow and Robert Udall, as they had all come to his rescue at some stage. All in all, the total amount owed by the departed to his family and friends came to a substantial proportion of his assets!

It is difficult to know just what the early Rogersett farms will have looked like at this stage, as none of the existing buildings here or elsewhere in the area are likely to pre-date the mid. sixteen hundreds. The usual materials for houses huddled up against the hillsides in such remote areas would have been wood and clay, and it is most likely that the old "cruck beam" structure would be used. But with such an abundance of rock and stone all around, it is probable that these would form much of the building as well. Roofs would remain thatched until well into the seventeenth century. Attached to, or very near, the main farmhouse would be the barns and other outhouses mentioned in the Percy Survey. Early structures to shelter the farmer's stock in winter would be just huts of clay or brushwood curved under a thatch of reeds or turves. Farm implements, as we see from other inventories, were very primitive. Simple ploughs were described in books written in the early 17th century: "The plough beam is the long tre above the which is a slight bente" (Fitzherbert), and, in Markham's "Boke of Husbandrie" the use of a plough staffe is defined: "they carry (the staffe) with the plough, and when the iron shilboard or plough beam be choaked with dirt, clay or filth, you shall put the same off the plough while going".

When not tending to their animals or cultivating their parcels of land, there was fuel to find for the fire. Tenants were given the right to dig peat and turf for burning, at certain times only. Peat was cut in May, when the hectic activity of lambing eased, and was transported on carts and wooden sledges.

List of debts owed by John Thwaite in 1596.

The peats would be stacked to dry and brought to the home in July. There were also strict rules about the harvesting of bracken on the hillsides. This could have been used as rough animal bedding or even fodder, and along with turf as roofing for the dwellings.

However industrious the Fischers, Maysons, Scotts and Walkthwaites may have been, there were two enemies they must have feared most of all. In Tudor England from time to time, plague and famine ravaged both town and countryside alike. By the time of the Survey, crisis was already looming in the north after successions of bad harvests and outbreaks of disease. Throughout the country rising prices had crippled the poor. The cost of living doubled between the years 1535-1570, and again by 1603. Famine and disease ravaged the north in 1586/7 and in 1597/9. To complete our picture of the Newlands farms in the sixteenth century, we need to think how drastically these hard times hit our families.

On a national level, during the next few years Elizabeth 1st was carefully and wisely consolidating her position as monarch of a rich and powerful nation. Dramatic events were unfolding in London and the South. In 1587 the unfortunate Mary Queen of Scots was finally beheaded at Fotheringay, at which news bonfires were lit in London. In the last months of 1588 the country rang with the news of the defeat of the Spanish Armada. Spanish ships were driven by storms around the north coasts of Scotland then down the west, where many were wrecked, not so many miles away from Newlands! But the Cumbrian farmers had far more pressing worries. In 1578 conditions were so bad in the North West that a Privy Council order was made for 1000 quarters of barley, oats and beans to be transported from Somerset and Dorset "for the sustentation of Her Majesty's subjects in Cumberland and Westmorland." Emergency rations such as these, however, would be destined for the towns, and would have no effect on life in the valleys, where each farmer would struggle to provide enough food and clothing for his own family.

The Crosthwaite Parish registers for the years of famine 1586/9 reflect the changes in daily life. From an average of 25 to 30 marriages a year, numbers dropped to 14 from May to December in 1586 with none during the winter, then just 12 from April to December in 1587. During that period however in Newlands, John Fysher of Snabb married Janet Peylle of Rogersyd, William Bonner of Rogersyd married Janet Scott of Birkryge, John Mayson of Newlands married Katherine Fysher, William Towlson of Keskaidell married Agnes Fysher (of Borrydell!) and Richard Fysher of

Snabb married Janet Towlson of Keskaidell. So we must conclude that not all aspects of life were grim! There was a great increase in the number of Crosthwaite burials, but these do seem to have affected mainly the townspeople of Keswick. Very many of the deaths were those of infants and "poore folk", reflecting perhaps starvation rather than pestilence. Several children and elderly folk of Newlands were buried at Crosthwaite, but the really dramatic rise in deaths did not come until the years 1597/9.

The century was to close with the worst disaster of all. A fierce outbreak of the plague began in the whole area in 1597. Letters and petitions from all over the North describe the suffering. The Calendar of State Papers records that "want and waste have crept into Northumberland, Westmoreland and Cumberland; many have to come 60 miles from Carlisle to Durham to buy bread,...corn has to be fetched from Newcastle, whereby the plague is spread in the northern counties." (Quoted in a paper by Henry Barnes in CWAAS, OS. Vol XI). And in a letter of Jan. 16th to the Queen's Secretary: "If corn were not brought in at Newcastle, which now has the plague, thousands would perish for want of bread." The Annals of Cartmel contained the following comment on the destructive effects of the weather at this time: "The cause of this destructive pestilence is thus described by King, in one of his sermons at York. "Remember the Spring was very unkind by means of the abundance of rains; our July hath been like a February, our June even as an April, so that the air must needs be corrupted. God amend it in His mercy and stay the plague of waters."

In Penrith there are still records of an ancient "Plague Stone". To quote again from Henry Barnes, a hollow in the stone was "about twelve inches square and ten inches deep, which was intended to hold some disinfecting liquid, most probably vinegar. In this trough the money from the hands of the townspeople was laid, and only when thus disinfected would the farmers receive it in payment for their goods." Near Keswick, on Armboth Fell, was a similar "Web Stone", and according to J. Fisher Crosthwaite in 1887 there was a legend that when the plague was in Keswick the country people came to "Cuddy Beck", where their produce was laid on the ground, then money was placed in the stream.

In Crosthwaite parish in 1597, 267 deaths were recorded. The usual average per year was nearer 30! The following year another 84 are registered, but there is reason to believe that this is not an accurate reflection of the real number of mortalities. A telling note by the vicar of Penrith, William Wallis, perhaps holds the key: "22nd day of September: Andrew Hodgson, a

The old oak sideboard at Low Snab, a wedding present to John and Issabell in 1643.

foreigner, (ie: not of the parish) was buried. Here begaune the plague, God's punishment in Penrith. All those that are noted with P died of the infection, and those noted F were buried on the fell". As we turn to the records for Newlands we have those grim words ringing in our ears. Just how many of the fathers, mothers and children of the hidden little farms had to bury their families in unrecorded graves on the hillsides? A legend is handed down amongst the Grave family at Skelgill, that a certain field wall above the farm sheltered the remains of victims of that family, who were hastily buried there without ceremony. Sure enough, a search of the Parish registers does fail to come up with the name Grave just at that time, even though there are dozens of those from other families!

As we search for familiar names among the officially recorded burials, it appears that certain families must have been living through unbearable grief. We return to the Thwaites of Rogersett. It is twenty five years since we met William and Janet Walkthwaite and their many children. The first part of the name Walkthwaite seems to have been dropped completely by the 1590s. The next generation of John and William had married local girls and were continuing to farm at Keskadale. Even Hugh Thwaite, mentioned as a child in William's will in 1574, had been married, to Elizabeth Yowdall, in 1590. In the cruel, raw cold of that winter of disease, the family lived through a time of unimaginable suffering. In one month alone, five of their number lost their lives:

.Dec. 1st William Thwaite. Dec. 3rd John Thwaite. Dec. 8th Esabell Thwaite. Dec. 14th Esabell Thwaite. Dec. 27 Margaret Thwaite. March 25th John Thwaite. Sept. 12th Agnes Thwaite.

At Birkrigg the Scots lost John, Christopher, Janet and Agnes. Several members of the Peele family, the Maysons and the Studdarts perished during these months, and at Gilbank the Fyshers who died included Janet, Richard, Nicholas, Robert and John! We even read of one of the German miners' families suffering in the tragedy: Symond Puphbarger had married Janet Fysher of Grange in 1575, and settled at Stare, where they had raised several children. The burials of '78/79 include Symond and his daughters Susan, Katheren and Margrette. Strangely, and perhaps ominously in the light of the vicar of Penrith's comments, there are no records of deaths among the Fyshers and Dovers of Snabb. Perhaps, they just barricaded themselves in to their hillside farm, as future registers would show that their dynasties continued, but it is more than likely that there are hidden bones deep beneath the fellside!

The tragic years of the plague end with the terrible record of the Bonners of Rogersyd. Living for many generations at this farmholding somewhere in the upper reaches of Newlands, the Bonners had featured regularly in births, deaths, marriages and court rolls. At least eight members of the family perished in the the outbreak: in July '97, Thomas and John, in August Agnes, another Agnes and William in September, and Richard ("wedow") with his infant daughter Margaret in February '98. The mention of the burial of Janet Bonner, infant, of "Littletowne", ten months later, in December 1598, adds a poignant codicile to the tragedy, with even that small ray of hope extinguished.

We will leave the valley at the end of the sixteenth century on a happier note. Once the pestilence began to subside, people picked up the pieces and life continued. Even in the thick of all the troubles, in August 1598, William Dover from Snabb had married Agnes Thwaite of Keskadell and moved in there. Agnes was the eldest daughter of John Thwaite, who died in 1576. In his will, he had passed the residue of his estate, after providing for Isobel his wife, to his three daughters. That William and Agnes both survived the next years is born out by the Baptism records of Anne and Elizabeth, their daughters, in 1599 and 1603.

1599 must have been a happier year for the farming families. At least four marriages were celebrated: John Clarke of Newlands and Elizabeth Bristow; William Maysone of Stoney Crofte and Jennet Maysone of Ussaker; John Fisher of Birkeryge and Elizabeth Fisher of Snabbe, and finally John Pufparker and Jennet Fisher. The German Pufparkers had made it into the next century!

Chapter 5
Commonwealth years: Life on the farm

The death of Queen Elizabeth 1st in 1603 heralded another period of political intrigue and religious upheaval in England and Scotland. The heir to the throne was James VIth of Scotland, son of the unfortunate Mary, Queen of Scots. The secret hope of English Catholics was that as James 1st of England he would revive that faith and support their cause. Although the King himself was more anxious to continue Elizabeth's reconciliatory policy, the country's deep feelings of hatred and suspicion of the "Papists" were re-ignited by the failed attempt of a group of fervent Catholics to blow up James and his whole parliament at Westminster in 1605.

Perhaps travelling peddlers and tradesmen brought to Keswick the amazing tale of Guido Faulkes and the gunpowder plot. The young men and women of Newlands may have joined in the bonfire celebrations for the King' deliverance as in other places all over the country. Their elders would have been obliged to read the New Thanksgiving service which was inserted into the prayer book and remained there until 1854. But no doubt what was of more significance to their daily life was the rebuilding of the family lines that

The 1647 lintel above the doorway at the old Stair Farm . A link with General Fairfax?

had been so devastated in the 1590s.

So, we can imagine the celebrations of the Thwaites of Keskadell, the Fyshers of Gilbank, the Bonners and Clarkes of Newlands, the Maysons of Rogerside, the Maysons of Skelgill and the Dovers of High Snabb, all of whom continued to marry and produce offspring in the years 1604/5.

There is no evidence of any dissension among the Anglican faithful of Crosthwaite parish. But in other parts of the country those most strongly opposed to the Papists had gone further, and even rejected the mid-way tolerance of the King. These people, known as "Puritans" for their extremely strict interpretation of the Scriptures and self-denying way of life, became almost as feared as the Catholics, and were also persecuted. During the first two decades of the 17th century many of them felt unable to live peacefully in England and joined the growing numbers of adventurers seeking a new life in the colonies. Looking back, we now speak of "The Pilgrim Fathers" who set sail from Plymouth in The Mayflower in 1620, but these happenings must have seemed very distant and unreal to the men of the Keswick area.

Just at that time, they were facing yet another period of soaring prices and failed harvests. Whilst the prices paid for wool in 1622 were at the lowest for fifty years, a report of the Privy Council in 1623 stated that "both in the North partes and in the Westerne partes of this realme the prizes of corne does yet remaine high and are likely to increase as the year growes on". Appleby, in "Famine in Tudor and Stuart England", points to evidence of starvation in the area. Not so far from Keswick, the parish records of Greystoke tell of the burials of "a poor fellowe destitute of succour", "a poore hugersterven beger childe" and "a poore beger striplinge" who died " in great miserie". Through all the towns and valleys, hundreds of beggars wandered searching for scraps of food.

The Crosthwaite parish records tell their own grim tale of death and suffering. Burials in 1623 rose from an average of around 50, to 256. What of the familiar Newlands names? It is strange to note that, amongst the hundreds of entries covering the town and all the nearby hamlets and rural communities, there are very few from our farm. Children, old people and the poorest do seem to have been most vulnerable in hard times. The Fishers, Studarts, Tollsons and Boners all lost infants. An unknown Elizabeth Taylour of Rogerside was described as "a poore widow", and Richard Stanger of Skelgill as a pauper. On May 24th the burial took place of Thomas Bowe of Millhowe (?) in Newlands, "senex nonagenarius"!

One very interesting burial was that of "Xpofer Scott, Curate at

Newlands Chappell, in ecclia" on 11th Oct. 1623. The chapel had existed in the heart of the valley for many years. In a later chapter we can look at the part it played in the local people's lives. But at this time, it is tempting to link "Xpofer" to the Scott family we have been following at Birkrigg. Was this a case of "local lad made good"? It would not have been an impossible achievement. In the late 1500s, records show that a foundation existed at the newly established Queens College, Oxford, for sons of poor families in Cumberland to be educated towards a career in the clergy. A Thomas Dover was vicar of Gilcrux in 1589, and James Dover of Cumberland matriculated at Queens in 1606, to later become Curate at Warcoppe. So we look for any other reference to the Scotts in Newlands at this time, and discover that on Oct. 7th 1621, the burial had taken place of "Elizabeth, wife of Sir Christofer Scott, Curate of Newlands Chappell". SIR Christofer! Had a son of the Birkrigg farmers really achieved a knighthood? Unlikely. At a later date, Bishop Nicholson informs us that almost every village curate was addressed as "Sir", without any necessary qualification. There were indeed two Christopher Scotts baptised in the Vale in the 1580s, but some twenty to thirty years later they both married lasses called Jennet. Not an Elizabeth in sight!

Back down in London, old King James 1st was dying. In 1625 his son was crowned Charles 1st and so began a time of unprecedented opposition to the role of the monarch and his nobles. Religious issues came to boiling point in Scotland, where an attempt by the king to enforce the use of the new Prayer Book resulted in a riot in St. Giles Cathedral in 1637. Not only religious issues had divided the country. Parliament itself, led by anti-royalists from the newly powerful middle classes, was challenging the king's authority. Tension grew and people started to take sides. The King's supporters, extravagant in their finery, their curling, flowing wigs, their arrogant attitude to the common people, still numbered amongst them the most powerful lords of the land. But under the influence of highly intellectual men of conviction like Pym and Hampton, the Parliamentarians gained strength. Charles in his arrogance had tried to rule without bowing to the demands of the elected representatives, but finally in 1640 he was obliged to re-call parliament. It was only a matter of time before the whole country was caught up in the Civil Wars.

The chief factor linking the remote North West in any way to these national events, was the involvement of the Landlord of most of the Newlands farms, Algernon Percy, 10th Earl of Northumberland. By 1640 the discontent of the Scots had manifested itself in the gathering of an army which had made its way as far as Newcastle. The Scottish generals declared

that they stood for liberty from oppression and appealed for aid fr
agreed with the Parliamentary and Puritan cause. The Earl was r
his support, but in Cumberland he was in a minority amongst tl.
tensions smouldered during the following year. In his capacity as Loru
Admiral of the King's fleet, Percy could have turned things in favour of the
monarch, but his exasperation and disappointment with the King's attitude led
him to favour a Parliamentarian, the Earl of Warwick, to command the fleet
in 1642. Events in London led to the flight of Charles and his Queen from
London to Hampton Court, and then further and further North until they
reached York. Meanwhile Parliament had delivered their 19 proposals for the
future government of the country, and lords and gentry all over the land were
forced to decide which side they supported. By the summer of 1642, the fuse
was ignited and years of bloody slaughter had begun. All over the land
families were torn apart by divided loyalties. The next few years saw
ferocious battles in both North and South.

Although the farmers of High Snab, Keskadale, Gilbank and
Stoneycroft probably continued with their struggle against the elements
scarcely affected by these upheavals, their links with the markets of Keswick
and Cockermouth, in buying and selling whatever commodities they needed,
and the tales of itinerant peddlers and craftsmen, must have made them aware
of the turmoil. When war finally broke out, they are unlikely to have been
counted as either "Roundheads" or, even less, as "Cavaliers"! The children
born to John and Anne Towellson of Keskadell, to John and Elizabeth
Mayson of Stonycroft, and to Christopher and Elizabeth Fisher of Littletown
in 1642 were to live the first twenty years of their lives during one of the
strangest periods in English history.

In 1648 the wars came uncomfortably close to this area. After five
years of fierce conflict, Algernon Percy of Northumberland had garrisoned
his castle at Cockermouth for the Parliamentary troops. It was the only
Roundhead stronghold in the area. As Royalist troops left the area for
Lancashire, Sir Marmaduke Langdale kept back 500 men to lay siege to the
castle. Word came to the new commander of the Roundheads, Oliver
Cromwell, who responded by dispatching a force under Lieut. Colonel
Ashton to relieve the besieged garrison, which he accomplished on 29th
September. According to contemporary accounts, the troops were very
orderly and well behaved in Cockermouth, and there were only eleven
casualties in the manoeuvre.

One of Cromwell's best and most well-loved generals was Sir Thomas

Fairfax, a Yorkshireman. In the village of Stair, in the centre of the Newlands valley, is an old farmhouse with a heavy stone door lintel, upon which are engraved the initials FF with the date 1647. Tradition has it that these are linked to Cromwell's leading general, Thomas Fairfax. A search of the Crosthwaite parish records for anyone of that name does reveal that a Thomas Fairfax of Caldbeck married Francis Parratt of Stare in 1628. It is therefore possible that FF was Francis Fairfax, but it seems strange that TF doesn't appear. Twenty years later a Grace Fairfax "of this parish", (their daughter?), married Thomas Stanick of Carlisle, in Dec. 1649. But, as these are the only Fairfax and Stanick/Stanwix entries for Crosthwaite, it is hard to find evidence to suggest that Sir Thomas Fairfax ever lived in the area, even after his retirement to Yorkshire to grow roses and write poetry! However, as these hearsay stories so often carry an echo of truth with them, it is intriguing to learn from a survey written over one hundred years later, by Nicolson and Burn the Historians, that in Stanger and Stare, a mile south of Braythwaite, "the late General Stanwicks had a small freehold estate"! Somewhere along the line there is a connection.

Various church records, however, do give us an insight into local life during the years of The Commonwealth, under Oliver Cromwell. In a purge of the Church of England, existing clergy were replaced by Puritanical ministers. From detailed accounts such as Walker's lists of "Suffering Clergy" and Calamy's "Ejected Ministers", as well as from our own church registers, we can discover what was happening in Crosthwaite Parish during the 1650s and 60s. One of the most disturbing changes for ordinary rural families, accustomed to following tradition, must have been the Act of Parliament passed in 1653. An entry in September of that year reads:

"Here endeth Marriages by a Minister in a Publique Manner".

Instead of the clergy, Justices of the Peace were to officiate at all births, marriages and burials. Subsequently we read: "December 6th. Thomas Williamson of Fieldside and Agnes Atkinson of Fornside both above ye age of 21 years, published three several Lord's Dayes and married by Mr. Henry Towlson Justice of the Peace according to an Act of Parliament dated 24th August 1653 and noe exception made to ye contrary wherefore ye said marriage should not beesoe solemnized." Mr. Towlson continued to oversee marriages until August 1654 when a Mr. Lancelot Fletcher of Tallentyre took over. In Newlands in 1654 the marriage took place between William Thwaite of Rogerside and Elizabeth Bonner of the same. Age-old family names, but under a new regime! In the Baptism registers too, we find reference to the

1653 Act, and an entry stating: "1654 Oct. 23rd Mr. Radcliffe enters as Vicar".

Percival Radcliffe had been appointed "Vicar of Crostwhaite in the County of Cumberland made to him by his Highness Oliver Lord Protector of ye Commonwealth of Engd." Percival's family were connected to the wealthy and influential Radcliffes of Derwentwater. Unfortunately, the Crosthwaite Church registers suffer a ten-year gap from 1658 to 1668, and during this time it is unclear what became of Percival Radcliffe.

The farmers of Newlands, however, did not need to travel as far as St. Kentigern's at Crosthwaite to hear the Word of the Lord! In 1652 "The Commisioners for propagating the Gospel in the 4 Northern Counties" had appointed James Cave as "Preacher at Crosby, Scaleby and Stanwix", with an allowance of £80 per. annum for maintenance, then, almost immediately, sent him on as an itinerant preacher at Thornthwaite, Newlands and St. John's with £104p.a. His appointment by the Commissioners was recorded on Nov. 3rd. 1652: "Whereas Mr. James Cave being recommended for a godly & painfull preacher & of able guifts & knowledge for the worke of ye Ministry & of approved conversation for piety hath come before us and upon tryall & examination of his guifts by divers godly Minrs. According to the direcon of the Parlt. Is found fitt to preach the Gospell of Jesus Christ." Mr. Cave was entitled for his support and maintenance to receive rents "menconed & conteyned in ye Schedule hereunto annexed", and his appointment was to be " lawfully Seised thereof to all intents and purposes as if he had bin instituted & inducted according to any forme or Course of Law & hath the like remedy for ye recovering thereof as ye deane and chapter of Carlisle formerly had".

The Justices of the Peace, however, held the licences for marriages etc. through the next few years. Justice Fletcher was followed by J.Ps Langhorne, Barwis and Wren. Some of them must have officiated at the baptisms of the Ozmotherley children. This very "foreign" sounding name was introduced into the valley when Henry Ozmotherley of Holme Coltrome married Anne Bowe of Newlands in 1651. Probably very few of the locals even knew where Holme Coltrome (now Cultram) was! For the next six years the Ozmotherleys of Uziker produced infants - Elinor, John, George and Robert, then completely disappeared from the registers. Presumably they had gone back to their foreign parts!

In April of 1657 another Newlands couple tied the knot: William Dover of Newlands and Agnes Towlson of Keskadel were married by Justice Hudson and "booked afterwards". They were followed by John Bell of High Snabb in Newlands and Isabell Fisher "of the same".

So life on the farms was continuing pretty much as always. This newly married William Dover was the great grandson of the first William, from Bassenthwaite, who arrived in 1574. Towlsons also had lived at Keskadale since the 1570s. The Percy Survey had listed a Robert Bell at Skelgill, and of course Isabell Fisher could have been a daughter of any number of Newlands families!

Then on October 30th 1657 comes a marriage registration which must have brought great joy to the valley; "Hugh Bowe of Swinside and Mabell Clocker of Parkside, by Mr. Radcliffe, our vicar"! Another Act of parliament that month had declared that "Now ministers are impowered to marrie again".

As has been mentioned, a long gap now occurs in the Crosthwaite registers. During this period, from 1658 until 1668, more momentous changes took place in the country. With the disintegration of the Commonwealth after the death of Oliver Cromwell, the monarchy was restored. On the 29th of May, 1660, Charles II entered London to wild scenes of rejoicing to take possession of the throne. Surely the distant Cumbrian families must have heard of the tumultous celebrations that day. The Diarist John Evelyn wrote of "above 20,000 horse and foote, brandishing their swords and shouting with inexpressible joy; the wayes strew'd with floweres, the bells ringing, the streets hung with tapistry, fountaines running with wine." Adulation and wild excitement reigned unchecked. Nearer to home, in Manchester and in Preston there are accounts of public days of thanksgiving, peals of bell-ringing, public feasts and bonfires with burning effigies of Cromwell.

At Cockermouth the Commonwealth-appointed Minister, George Larkham, now ejected from his post, wrote that on May 2Ist "Rex Carolus the Second was proclaimed at Cockermouth, with the great triumphing of many wicked men."

We will leave the wider field of national events now and return to some very revealing insights into life on the farms. Although the parish registers fail us for the next few years, we do have copies of the wills and inventories of some of the Fishers, Dovers, Cowpers, Scotts and Maysons who died at this time. The details in these suggest that gradually some of the families were improving their lot and accumulating more basic household furniture and implements.

In the will of Isabell Dover, widow of William of High Snab, in 1661, there is little indication of any material or financial prosperity. William, who had died in 1637, had left his "riding geare and plowe geare" to his son, William. Isabell is able to pass on to her daughter and grandchildren several modest sums of money, sometimes with the addition of "one gimmer".

Gimmer is the old norse dialect name for a one year old ewe, so the younger grandchildren were probably receiving them as a token gift, or even as pets! Another elderly lady of Newlands died the same year: in the will of Agnes Fisher we read not only of five shillings and one cow, going to her daughter, but of "our new bed standing in the Inner Chamber", a bequest to her son Robert.

John Cowper, who also died in Newlands in 1661 had accumulated a total sum of £120, a fair amount in those days, which he divided between his daughters. His son John inherited all the usual "husbandry geare", along with the "Long Croft", the "greate Arke", and the table in the house.

In 1662, however, we come to some more interesting items. The first is the will of Hugh Mayson. In his bequests there is nothing unusual. He leaves unto his son John all the "husbandry geare, plowgeare and ridding-geare". His son-in-law Robert Fisher gets "tow shillings & six pence", and the residue of his goods goes to Katherin his wife and Agnes his daughter. In the inventory which followed after his death, however, we get a fascinating insight into the possessions and general lifestyle of this fairly typical Newlands farmer.

Hugh was probably the son born in 1585 to Henry Mason of Snabb and his wife Katheren, although there were other Hugh Maysons around at that time. His son John, chief inheritor in his will, was born in 1630, just recorded as in "Newlands", but the place of his daughter Agnes' birth in 1638 was registered as Littletowne. This movement around the farms, often linked to the size of the flocks of sheep, was by no means unusual at that time. With Maysons by now at Keskadell, Stonicroft and "Eakin" (now Akin), we can assume that the family had been prospering. The "Fower sworn men" signing the inventory were William Jinkinson of Buttermire, Robert Ffisher, William Dover and Hugh Wren of Newlands. The first item on the list was "His appareil; prized to £1-10-00". Hugh would hardly have had a sartorial line in clothing! As in all the families, everyday wear would have been homespun, using the very coarse Herdwick wool producing thick, rough garments.

The bedding and linen that follow show a certain degree of night-time comfort, and the various pewter, stone and wooden "vessells" would be for everyday use at the table and in storage. An important entry comes next: "Chests and Arkes", valuable items worth £3-10-00. They were the safe storage for clothing and anything of value. No doubt roughly made and unadorned at this early stage, they were nevertheless proudly handed down from one generation to another. The other items of furniture mentioned are

The Inventory of Hugh Mayson, 1662, tells us much about day-to-day life on the farm.

chaires, chambres, stooles, cradle and "frame in the house side". This last item features in many inventories, and was possibly a weaving frame, used by the womenfolk, Agnes and her daughters, in cloth-making. This is suggested too by the "Whiele and Carder" next in the list. After "fower ladders" we come to the Barke, a box containing home-made rush candles. A "winnowcloth", mentioned before we read of the store of grain, reminds us of the essential annual activity of winnowing the grain by hand, throwing it into the wind and catching the heavier grain as it separated from the chaff.

Hugh had left a store of "Bigge, Meale, Malt and Groats", worth £2-00-00, the staple diet of the customary tenant. Bigge was a poor quality type of oats, grown on the stoney ground around each farm. Almost all meals would contain some form of porridge and oat-cakes made from their limited supplies. The next few items relate to the cooking and baking processes: "Girdle & Brandreth, Crooke & Tongs". These would be used in the making of haver or clap bread, made from bigge or oats and resembling Norwegian flatbrod. The large iron girdle was supported on the tripod, the brandreth or brandiron, about 8 inches high, over the hearth. We have a detailed account of the work involved in clap-bread making from Celia Fiennes, an enterprising lady of the late 17th century who journeyed around the Lake District on horseback. Although her observations were made in a farmhouse in Kendal, in 1698, we can tell from our inventories that equipment and therefore methods were just about the same up in the Northern valleys:" They mix their flour with water so soft as to rowle it in their hands into a ball, and then they have a board made round and something hollow in the middle riseing by degrees all round to the edge a little higher, but so little as one would take it to be a board warp'd, this is to cast out the cake thinn and so they clap it round and drive it to the edge in a due proportion till drove as thinn as paper, and still they clap and drive it round, and then they have a plaite of iron same size with their clap board and so shove off the cake on it and so set it on coales and bake it…if their iron plate is smooth and they take care their coales or embers are not too hot but just to make it look yellow it will bake and be as crisp and pleasant to eate as anything you can imagine."

While the ladies were busy with their cloth-weaving and baking, Hugh and his sons and labourers would be attending to the most important aspect of their livelihood, the animals. Reading on into his inventory, we come to Cattell, tow Mares and Sheepe, with a total value of £51-05-08, far more than everything else put together. It is clear from many other inventories of the period that the farmers owned large numbers of cattle as well as sheep. The mention of butter and cheese reminds us that all farmsteads had their butteries, in outhouses or as an extension of the main house, where rowan branches and garlands would be hung to ward off the evil spirits that spoiled the churning. The final, humble members of Hugh Mayson's farm were the cocks and hens, adding the last one shilling to the total value of Hugh's possessions, £77-02-00, a reasonable amount for the time. Other farmers in the valley were not as fortunate: Henry Mayson, from a different branch of the family, died a few years later leaving only £15-15-04. But in April of 1662 the inventory of James Dover of Swinside revealed assets of £133-04-08. He and his family had enjoyed slightly more comfort than the Maysons, as born out by the listing of "Quishens" (cushions), tablecloth and bookes. Sheep worth £37-04-00 indicated a larger flock than Hugh Mayson's. In the course of the last thirty years of the century, other Newlands families continued to prosper. John Cowper of High Snabb owned household and farming goods worth £163 in 1678, and those of John Thwaite in 1684 were valued at £125. Several other farmers, however, just managed to make ends meet, leaving possessions of only twenty to forty pounds.

Even so, life in the harsh countryside must have been preferable to the misery in London during the outbreak of plague in 1666. Far away from the filth and squalor of the diseased city, where the pestilence raged so fiercely that at its height seven thousand people died in one week, the population of Newlands was growing, and new buildings were appearing. When they heard about the great fire of London in September of the same year, it would be hardly possible for the Thwaites and Fishers to imagine the destruction of St. Paul's Cathedral and of thirteen thousand dwelling houses and eighty nine churches! Their own concerns were focussed on repairing and expanding their dilapidated farm buildings, and in many instances building entirely new dwelling houses for the next generation.

From Swinside farm, the will and inventory of John Dover, 1704, compared with the earlier ones of his father James in 1662, reveal the extent to which some of the more successful farmers were able to improve life for themselves and their families by the turn of the century.

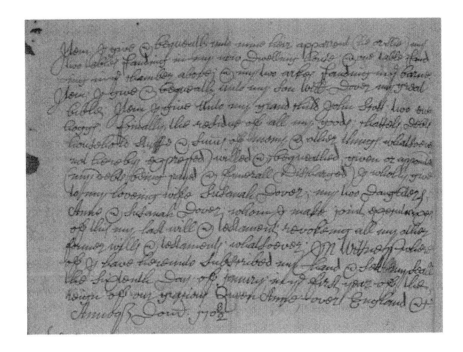

Chapter 6
Prosperity and Property

Anyone wandering around the narrow roads, lanes and farm-tracks of Newlands today finds a different farmhouse with almost every bend. Some, like High Snab and Birkrigg, stand out bright and clear, their whitewashed walls gleaming when the sun manages to shine over the heights of Maiden Moor and High Spy. Others, Low Snab perhaps or Gillbrow, are huddled up under the hillside and only the more determined walkers will find them. Two or three are so well hidden that only a chosen few know that they are there. These, as in the case of Low High Snab or Low House, are among the oldest existing buildings in the Valley. It is very difficult now to visualise exactly how they looked in 1700, but some of them definitely owe their present structure to foundations laid in the "Great Re-building".

A study of the wills of two generations of Dovers illustrates very

Above: John Dover leaves a new house and possessions to his 'beloved wife Susanah' and family.

The ancient walls of Low Skelgill Farm, home of generations of the Grave family. The present Mr and Mrs Grave are standing in the doorway.

clearly what was happening during the last few years of the seventeenth century.

James Dover of Swinside died in 1662, the same year as Hugh Mayson whose inventory we have already examined. James' inventory is very similar to Hugh's. Their basic household equipment is the same, though a few items indicate that the Dovers were possibly a little more prosperous than the Maysons. So, we read that James Dover owned a flock of sheep valued at £37-0-0, cows at £34-0-0, kept bees worth 18s-00d and passed on 8s-00 worth of books. However, when his son John died in 1703, still at Swinside, the buildings he had inherited had been transformed.

It was a phenomenon of these years that all over the county farmers were able to repair and extend their dilapidated farmhouses and outbuildings to meet the needs of growing families and larger stocks of animals. When we read John Dover's will and inventory we learn not only of his "moveable" possessions, but also details of which rooms they were in. In the will, the most significant remark is:

"Item: I give and bequeath unto my heir apparent (he or she) my two tables standing in my new dwelling house and one table standing in the chamber above." Between 1662 and 1703 great changes had taken place. John also mentions "my freehold lands which I purchased of John Bowe of

Swinside", a reminder that more than one family lived in the group of tenement buildings, as well as indicating the comparative wealth of John Dover.

Before this period of development, most of the Newlands/Rogersett farmsteads would have been of a basic two-unit plan, with out-houses and barns. Studies by the historian Professor Brunskill and others have illustrated that although there would be several variations in lay-out, in most farms the main living area known simply as "the house" or "fire-house", would be separated from the "chamber", where the farmer and his wife slept, by a central passage running from front to back. Everyone else in the household, children and labourers, would sleep together in the open loft, reached by a step-ladder, on boards fastened to the beams of the roof.

John Dover, like so many Yeomen farmers of his generation, provided more privacy for his family and more convenient working areas. Virtually independent, free from interference of landlords, the men of the Cumbrian valleys became known as "Statesmen", each with his own small "estate". We know of this re-building period not only from inventories but from the visible evidence of heavy stone door lintels bearing initials and dates on old farm buildings all over the area. Many Newlands farms were of the "long-house" style. With the back of the farm hugging the hillside, additional rooms were built at one end, or the byre was converted into living space and new out-buildings constructed. Walls were raised and the roof pitch altered to create new chambers, reached by more substantial staircases.

Turning to the details in the Dover inventory we see the extent of his improvements: items were valued in "the farr loft . . . the nexte roome . . . another roome . . . the next roome. . . . The false loft . . . he Parlour roome . . . the Buttry . . . the milkhouse . . . the bodystead of the house . . . the pantry . . . the Bowe-house . . . the barn and out-houses."

In this luxury accommodation lived John and his "beloved wife" Susanah with their family, John, Mary, An, James, William and Joseph, though not all survived childhood. But in reality, life would be far from luxurious! Whilst all the re-building was taking place, the daily struggle to survive continued. Large flocks of sheep and herds of cattle were to be cared for. In 1662, James Dover had cattle and horses worth £75-0-0, whereas John's livestock in 1703 was valued at £153-0-0. All other aspects of farming life continued with primitive machinery and much hand-labour. Oats were sown in the spring, arable land was managed for grazing then left for the "fog"- coarse hay- to be reaped later in the year. Peat was cut from the Moss and stored for fuel, and bracken was harvested for animal (and sometimes human) bedding or thatching.

Other farms in Newlands even today retain essential features of these early alterations and extensions. At Low Skelgill the long low building almost hidden against the hillside is still the home of the Grave family, whose forebears shared life in that hillside community with the Bells, Tickells and Fishers. The ancient stones of the hay barn and bracken barn stand firm, while inside the house, the thick walls, various floor levels, old beams and narrow staircases, even after extensive changes, conjure up a vivid picture of the family dwelling in the seventeen and eighteen hundreds. Looking today at the ancient stones and low roofs of Low Snabb farm we can easily imagine William Fisher in 1726 bequeathing unto "my beloved wife Isabell the sum of ten pounds and all the bedding, pewter and wooden vessels, two iron potts one chest and an ark and one cow and one chair"! His daughter Mary received fifty pounds, Leonard Pearson and his wife Elizabeth (William's daughter) five shillings, and "unto their children every one, two shillings and sixpence a piece." The farmhouse, probably looking very much as it does now, with its typical contents and basic furnishings, was passed on to William's son Joseph. He also became the proud possessor of a flock of sheep worth £50, cattle and horses at £20 and corn and hay (already harvested as this was in October) to the value of £15. The inventory of the farm contents was then witnessed by Leonard Pearson, Robert Fisher of Skellgill, Lancelot Fisher and John Scott of Newlands. This John was a force to be reckoned with. Six years earlier he had lodged a complaint at the Manor court against William Fisher, and two years after that he had played an important part in the life of William Dover, as we shall see later.

Communications between farms and towns in this isolated location must have been more difficult than we can imagine. Now, in the 21st century, with our tarmac roads and drainage, heavy rain and wind still causes flooding and obstruction. In those days of stones and mud, journeys must have been horrendous, even on the main highways. Bouch and Jones, in "The Lake Counties 1500 to 1830", quote three 17th century Southerners, travelling from Penrith to Kendal: "Through such ways as we hope wee neuer shall againe, being no other but climing, and stony, nothing but Bogs and Myres, or the tops of those high Hills, so as we were enforc'd to keepe these narrow, loose, stony, base wayes . . . if a man marke not his way very well and so chance to be out a wee bit, the rude, rusticall and ill-bred People, with their gainging and yating, have not will . . . enough to put us in; we could not vnderstand them, neither would they vnderstand us." These "rude, rusticall and ill-bred people", however, were doing the best they could to improve conditions.

In Chapter Two we saw that even in the 15th century, Acts of Parliament had laid down regulations for local men to take on responsibilities for the maintenance of roads, hedges and ditches. These unpaid surveyors had to be appointed in each parish and if necessary order householders to put in six days a year working on the roadways. The Manorial court records from Cockermouth Castle, which gave us the insights into fifteenth century organisation and practice, continue for the next two hundred years. At these courts, the individual Manors of Braithwaite and Coledale, Newlands, and Portinscale comprised the Great Manor of the Derwent Fells. Justices of the Peace appointed men from each area to oversee the carrying out of the Byelaws, acting as Surveyors, Sessors, Constables and "Lookers". From surviving records of the Quarter Sessions of the Court Leet, we discover which of our farmers had to take on these duties from time to time.

At the Court Leet held on April 27th 1678 the following appointments were made:

"Sessors" for Newlands: John Bowe and Christopher Ffisher.

Constable for Newlands: Robert Ffisher

Hedge Lookers for Newlands: John Couper and John Thwaite

Mill Grinder for Rogerside: John Scott of Birkrigg

These men would in theory be responsible for general law and order in the community, and for the reporting of any neglect in hedge and ditch maintenance. A group of Jurors were appointed to decide on penalties for anyone found guilty of minor transgressions. On April 27th for example, Gavin Scott was ordered to repair a defective bridge "betwixt 7th and 10th of May".

The Jurors' names in that year are now very familiar to us: two hundred years earlier men of the same names had also been called upon to serve the community in this way:

Joseph Tickell - Scalegill (Skelgill)

Gawin Scott - Gt. Braithwaite

Hugh Towlson - Keskidell

Joseph Thwaite - Keskidell

William Dover - Newlands (a cousin of John, living at Snab)

Joseph Bowe - Newlands

Robert Ffisher - Newlands

John Mayson - Aykin

John Harriman

Any official decisions were declared to be "put in paine". So, a few years later, we read that "It is put in paine that those of Skelgill and Gillbank and the rest doth make the bridge at Gilbank within 4 days and putt the same in goode repair".

Whilst small offences or acts of neglect were dealt with on this very local level at the Court Leet, more general matters concerning the community were settled at the Manor court in Cockermouth. When a customary tenant died or grew too old to manage his estate, the lands and the flocks of sheep were passed down to an heir apparent. An appearance at the Court was required for the legal transfer of the property. In 1677 we meet John Dover again, when he was appointed heir to his mother Elizabeth Dover. His father James as we know had died in 1662, so John had been helping his widowed mother on the farm for fifteen years. As she grew too frail, he finally took over the tenancy. She died in 1681.

Sometimes the decrees of the manor court affected the whole community. From the Cockermouth documents dated 1690 we discover that "as several within that neighbourhood (Littletown, Skelgill and Hawse End) hath been very negligent when desired to goe to hunte ye fox, everyone having sheep on the fells there is, on notice, to send a man to hunt on paine of 12d." In 1690 the law commanded involvement in fox-hunting: over three hundred years later the same activity has been outlawed!

While the courts dealt with such a wide variety of matters, there was still one other way in which grievances could be settled. From Cockermouth again we learn of the "Petitions to the Lord". Occasionally in Newlands as in any community, disputes would arise which needed more individual attention. The "lord" in question in the 1600s was Algernon Percy, 10th Earl of Northumberland. Tenants with a personal complaint against a neighbour, or perhaps a group of men feeling ill-used by the lord's officials, could send a formal letter of complaint to his lordship through his commissioners. Amazingly, some of these letters still survive.

The earliest such letter from Newlands is dated 1597. It was sent by Robert Fisher "on behalf of the tenants of Rogersett or Newlands". (Note the parallel use of the names at this stage.) Casting our minds back to 1597, we remember that plague and famine were raging at that time, but Robert, probably one of the Fishers living at Snab, took the lead in trying to keep things going. His complaint was that they had been "dispossessed by the lord's officers of the tenant right of Newlands Mill". The mill in question could have been the corn mill at Stair, probably the same one mentioned in the court roll of 1522. In return for a fee, at that time £10, certain tenants were given the right to grind everyone's corn at the mill. Perhaps the officers interfering in the system were making off with flour for themselves! We have no record of the outcome of the case, but presumably the tenants' rights were restored, as there is frequent mention of the mill at later dates.

Whilst thinking of the corn mills, we can read another account, surviving in a very delicate state amongst the Cockermouth papers. It refers to a mill in Braithwaite, not Newlands, but tells us of typical everyday problems. Addressed to their Graces the "Duke and Duchess of Sumersett", the letter was therefore written after 1682, at which time Elizabeth, the Percy heiress, had married Charles Seymour, Duke of Somerset. It is worth reading in full:

"The humble Petition of Joseph Tickell, John Dover, John Birkett, Robert Bowe and John Wilkinson, their Graces' tennants in Braithwaite . . . they Humbly showeth . . . that whereas your petitioners did sometime heretofore during the time of Mr. Boach being commissioner did take to farme of their Graces their Water Corn Mill at Braithwaite aforesaid under the yearly rent of tenn pounds and with Covenants to make necessary repairs. . . That your Petitioners have accordingly done all that within them lyes, to keep the said Millne in repair, but she, being soe old a building, and the maine walls soe extreamly in decay and become soe very crazy that it is not possible to support her with-out rebuilding for that the walls will not admitt of any patching or reparacon. Wherefore the Premises considered, your Petitioners desire your immediate direcon therein, so that she may not suffer for want of timely care."

One hopes that the corn mill in question appreciated all the loving care she received.

To return to the farmers of Newlands. Inevitably the Maysons soon turn up! In an undated petition, William Mayson of Stonicroft protests against Leonard Parrett, who apparently is preventing William from irrigating his land, and failing to repair his hedgerows. (petition no. 23). Apart from studying the style of writing in the petition, an easier way of dating it is to search for this previously unheard-of name, Parrett, in the parish registers. There he is, in a baptismal entry in 1611: "Francis, daughter of Leonard Parratt of Stare, and Jennett." In June 1628, Thomas Fairfax of Caldbeck married this Francis, when she was only 17. At that point she must have gone to live in Caldbeck as there are no further references to the union. Nor do there seem to have been any more Parratt children baptised in the parish, as the only other entry for the family is the burial of Leonard, still from "Staire",

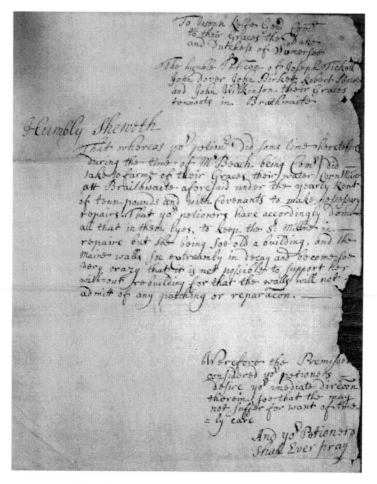

A very humble group of petitioners plead for their mill.

in May 1645. We can therefore assume that William's protest was made at some time between 1620 and 1640.

One other tenant in nearby Braithwaite deserves a mention. In 1654, poor old Gawin Bowe was in trouble. In petition no. 343 we read his request to the commissioners for the Earl of Northumberland: he claims that "Whereas this last sumer he was forced to build anew his mansion house at Brathwaite aforesaid, and bought all the wood for the same, to his great hardship. And now of laite in a greate storme when the walls were green and the timber scarce setled, the chimneys thrust downe upon the timber and broke it, so as it is not possible…Your petitioner therefore prayes that your Worships will be pleased to allow him some timber-woode out of Fall Parke for building his house again, he being a very poore man is not able to build it again."

Do not be mislead by the word "mansion"; at that time, it simply denoted "dwelling house". A scribbled note at the bottom of the letter tells us that at least some sympathy was shown: a warrant was granted for Gawin to take timber from "the upperside in Brathwaite".

The most intriguing petition of the later 1600s is undated, but contains the signatures (or "marks") of no fewer than 21 Newlands farmers. The villain of the piece is one John Gaskarth of "Gudderskell". Gutherscale, as it is now, is a well-hidden farmhouse on the Northern slopes of Catbells. With Skelgill and Hawse End it was a link on the route from the valley to Portinscale and on to Keswick. In 1604, Cuthbert Gaskarth had married into the Bowe family, long-time residents of Gaskarth, and his son John was carrying on the family name. The petition, from William Stanger and John Nixon, was addressed to the Worshipful William Pennington Esquire, his Lordship's Lieutenant, and the rest of the Commissioners. The Stangers had been around for several generations, some working for the German miners in 1570s. The only reference to John Nixon in the parish registers is that he died in Keswick in 1670.

The humble Petitioners declared that "one John Gaskarth of Gudderskell hath inclosed a parcell of his Lordship's Comon within the Manner of Brathwt and Cowdall called Brodehow, being about an acre of ground…which is to the comon anoyance of manye of his Lordship's tenantes therbye dwelling, for that the petitioners and manye others have a highe way throwe the said ground, both to churche and markett; and a comon waye for your petitioners and others to drive ther goodes to and from the Comon, and a place which is a downe fall for sheepe in a storme.

May it please your good Worships not to suffer the said ground to be inclosed, but that it may be as it formerly late bene, and your petitioners shall ever pray etc.

Richard Ffisher	John Rawling	Edward Harryman
William Studdart	John Ffisher	John Ffisher
Hugh Ffisher	John Cowper	John Harriman
Henery Ffisher	John Bowe	John Berkete
John Twaith	John Scott	Christopher Birkett
John Mayson	Robert Bowe	Robert Bell
William Twaith	Richard Bell	John Birket

To the wo: Willm Pennington esquire his Lo:[rd]
Lowe tenante and the rest of his Lo:[rd]
Comissione

The humble peticion of within Glangow John Riger
and of his his Lo:[rd] tenanty

Humbly showeth unto yo[ur] wor[ship] that one John Hubbart of
Hudderston hath inclosed a peece of his Lo[rd] Comon within
the Manner of Bratyet & Sowdale, called Woodehowse
bonage about an acre of ground (well wall) & to be sold
also to the Comon anoiance of many of his lord=
shipe tente hereto his dwelliнge for that peti; and when
offred have a hitte way granted the said ground both
to Church & Markett, and to Comon whop for yo[ur] selfe
& ought to drive her goods to & from the Comon, &
a place which a downe fall for her sheepe in a Storme:

May it please yo[ur] good wor[ship] not to suffer the said
ground to be inclosed, but that it may be had it
formerly hath bene, and yo[ur] peti[tioners] shall
ever pray &c:

Richard Fisher
William Stuedare
Hugh Fisher

Henry Fisher   Robert Bowe
John Tomich   Richard Bell
John Mayson   Edward Harryman
William .....   John Fisher
                                John Hammon
Jean Rawling   John Bowe
John Fisher   Christopher Durbell
John Cooper
John Bowe   Robert Wod
John Prott   John Richard

Although we have no date on the petition, a study of these signatories in the parish records links them to Newlands farms around 1650-1660. With no fewer than four Ffishers adding their names to the protest, we can trace them to Gilbank and Low Snab. John Scott was at Birkrigg, John Cowper at High Snab and John Mayson at Ekine (Akin). The Bells were at Skelgill, the Harrymans and Birketts at Portinscale. Significantly, Richard Bell and William Studdart died in 1670, the same year as John Nixon, leaving the likely time of the petition as around 1660.

Details of the complaint shed interesting light on the situation in the valley. The enclosed parcel of land was part of his lordship's common "within the manner of Brathwt and Cowdale". Our present Coledale is a corruption of the original name of the smaller valley above Braithwaite, known as Cowdale until the later 1800s. The church in question would be St. Kentigern's at Crosthwaite, and the market would be in Keswick, both important places in the countrymen's lives. The reference to the "inclosure" of land reflects the growing need in the 17th century for defined boundaries around land and properties, as more of the common lands, often bogs and mosses, were reclaimed for arable purposes. Our petitioners were probably typical of many tenant farmers in Cumbria who struggled to sort out the legalities of new enclosures. Sadly, we have no record of the response of William Pennington, but doubtless there would be many other similar thorny problems for our farmers in the years ahead.

Another farmer who found himself in trouble at this time was Richard Tickell, of Skelgill or Ullock. In the first year of the reign of William and Mary, 1689, he was summonsed to the court at Cockermouth to face charges from the Duke and Duchess of Somerset relating to the illegal cutting and selling of wood. In his defence a worthy band of parishioners testified that, from times "beyond memory", they had been allowed to " take and carry away without molestation" certain underwoods of oak, ash, alder and birch. JohnTickell of Skelgill aged 60, David Davis of Staire aged 48, John Rowland of Newlands aged 57 and William Fisher of Gutterskill aged 56, were amongst those questioned by the commissioners.

Moving firmly into the 18th century, our final petition is dated 1711. This one provides evidence that felling of trees in Newlands as in all lowland areas of Cumbria had escalated to unsustainable proportions. A certificate with ten signatures supported Joseph Bell of Rogersett, (actually living at Skelgill), in his claim that such a large number of trees had been cut down from his tenements "for the purpose of repairs to Cockermouth Castle", and various other repairs, that he had no longer sufficient timber to deal with repairs to his own property, "despite the fact that some 40 ago his father had purchased from the Lord of the Manor rights to cut timber on his own land". The friends and neighbours supporting him were the sons of those we met in the Gutherscale petition! We know that from the twelfth century onwards, the richly wooded fells and dales of Cumberland fell victim to the axes and saws of generations of charcoal burners, monks, miners, house-builders and landed gentry. The repairs referred to in Joseph Bell's plea had been occasioned by the sacking and neglect of Cockermouth Castle after the Civil Wars.

It seems as though the early eighteenth century brought with it a fiercer need to fight for one's rights and stake a claim to lands and highways. Perhaps with more sons surviving, farmers' families were spreading out and struggling to define their boundaries. Thus, in the beautifully scripted records of the Manor Court in Braithwaite in 1720 we read not only of those appointed jurors etc. but of several disputes in the valley. Gawin Scott, John Harriman, Robert Ffisher, William Thwaite had to reach verdicts on such problems as:

" William Dover complains of Joseph Clarke, Francis Ratcliffe and George Barwick for want of a way to his Coledale Moss." The decision was that William Dover should have a way to Cowdale Moss (note the use of both names) from Braithwaite by the Peat Land through George Barwick's Moss, building himself a bridge.

Thomas Bowe of Newlands complained that John Towlson of Keskadale was going through "the low end of the gill", and John Scott of Gill Brow brought a case against William Fisher of the Low Snab for "driving his sheep onto the Lowe road and claiming a Sheep Heaf on The Tongue". These local court hearings were obviously of great importance at the time. We have evidence too that the occupancy of the farms changed frequently. The baptisms of children born to one and the same couple were often registered from different farms. Some meticulously scribed Indentures, recording transfers of "Customary Tenure", or ownership of the lease, still survive today. Among them is one from 1722, referring to High Snab.

We have been following the fortunes of different families in the community at "Snab". It has become apparent that there were, from early times, several farmsteads dotted around this hillside area below the ridge, or tongue, of upland known as The Snab. In the course of the fifteen hundreds we have seen Thomas Scott, John Fischer, John Tollynson, Thomas Maison, Hugh Fyscher, William Dover and Samuel Clerke all mentioned at some time living at Snabb. In the German mining accounts, we also learned that some of

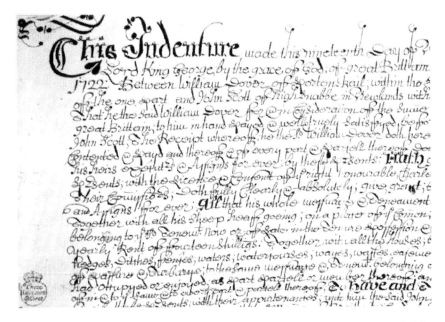

The beautifully scripted Indenture for the sale of High Snab Farm in 1722

those named were actually at "Low Schnap", whereas the will of William Dover in 1637 firmly places him at "High Snabb". As there is also a farm at "Low High Snab", it can be quite difficult to sort them out. However, records show that in 1715, the sixth William Dover to live at High Snabb continued the family name there when he married a Jane Fisher. It seems, though, that after a couple of years they moved to Skelgill, (then within in the boundaries of Portinscale), where some of their children were born. The old document now at Carlisle Records Office, is part of a collection deposited by the National trust when they took over ownership of the farm in 1969.

In a wonderfully clear "Secretary Hand", the Indenture was made "this nineteenth day of November in the ninth year of the reign of our Sovereign Lord King George.........between William Dover of Portonskeil within the Parish of Crosthwaite in the County of Cumberland, Yeoman, of the one part, and John Scott of High Snabbe in Newlands in the parish aforesaid, Yeoman, of the other part." We now read a daunting legal settlement whereby William Dover sells, for the sum of Two Hundred and Sixty Pounds "of good and lawful money of Great Britain", (surely a fortune in those days!) the customary tenure of High Snab Farm. As we thread our way through the mass

High Snab in winter. A tough place for farmers and sheep alike.

of legal jargon, repetition and minute detail, we sense the ancient tradition of these agreements.

He, "with the licence and consent of the Right Honorable Charles Duke of Sumersett, Elizabeth his wife, Duchesse of Sumersett and their comissioners, doth fully, clearly and absolutely give, grant, bargain sell and surrender unto him the said John Scott, his heirs and assigns for ever, all that his whole Messuage and Tenement situate, lying and being at High Snabbe in Newlands aforesaid, together with all his Sheep Heafe, goeing on a place of the Comon, commonly called and known by the name of Littledalehead and thereabouts, belonging to the said tenant, now and of late in the tenure and possession of him the said William Dover or his Assigns, being of the yearly rent of fourteen shillings; together with all the houses, buildings, gardens, orchards, crofts and lands, whatsoever hedges, ditches, fences, waters, watercourses, easements, woods, underwoods, moores mosses; Sheep Heafes ,Commons, Pastures and Turbage...........to Have and to Hold the afforesaid Messuage and tenement and all the other premises.....unto the said John Scott, his heirs and Assigns for ever, according to the Custom of Tenant Right now used and allowed within the Manor of Braithwaite and Cowdale, yeilding and paying therefore Yearly unto the said Charles Duke of

Sumersett, Elizabeth his Wife, their heirs and Assigns, or to their Officer or Officers, the yearly rent of 14s. at the Feasts and termes due for right to be payed, and doing and performing all other duties and services of right due accustomed to be done for the same". Etc.

In this way the Scott family established their rights at High Snab. John may well have borrowed money to help him at this stage - many inventories of the time include substantial lists of creditors and debtors - but basically he was doing well. John died in 1738 and in his will passed on his farm to his son George. His wife, still living in High Snab, inherited "the Red Cowe and tow Loads of Oatmeall this Year and one load next Year and five stone of wool."To his grandson John went Cupboards, a Tressle table, "tow Arkes in the Barne and tow Ews going upon The Rigg".

From the documents deposited by the National Trust we can follow the subsequent negotiations at High Snab. Alongside the Scotts, the Cowpers had also been living at High Snab for a few generations. Deeds of Enfranchisement were made in 1759 between Charles Earl of Egremont, by then the Landlord, George Scott and John Cowper. George bought his share of the holding for £202-13-7. As we will see in later chapters, from the mid-1700s onwards properties changed hands, and family members moved out of the valley to find new livings. The Scotts and Cowpers continued to hand on ownership of High Snab to their descendants, in one case a John Scott of Workington, Inn Keeper, and in another a Rev. Thomas Cowper of Bargate in the Parish of Loweswater.

One final twist in the tale: a hundred years later, in 1873, Richard Woodward Esq. sold High Snab Farm to Mr. Moses Dover for £2,110. The Dovers had returned to their original dwelling-place, three hundred years after William arrived from Bassenthwaite!

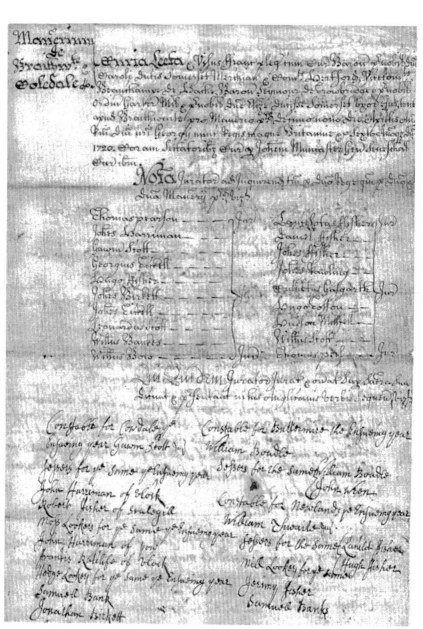

Constables, Lookers and Jurors in Braithwaite District, 1720.

Chapter 7
Legal Proceedings

We have moved into the eighteenth century, yet still we follow the fortunes of the Fishers, Dovers, Scotts, Thwaites and Tolsons, the descendants of the seventeenth century farmers. With the increase in literacy, the determination to fight unjust procedures, and the strong community spirit in Newlands, we can read in depositions, petitions and wills, more and more details of farming life and the fight for ancient rights. Alongside, we hear of sales of property, new names in the farmsteads and a dispersion of the younger generations.

Early in the century, the Manor Courts still appointed the "Constables"and "Lookers"for the area, and demanded the services of several farmers at a time as Jurors. A page beautifully written in Latin in 1720 gives us the names of the Jurors for the court Leet of Braithwaite and Coledale. It is no surprise that here we meet the sons of the 1678 Sessors, Constables, Lookers and Grinders. The Harrimans, Thwaites, Ffishers and Bowes were still looking after their Valley.

But not all grievances were settled in local courts. A most fascinating document is held in the National Archives at Kew. On a collection of large waxy sheets we can read the original records of the clerk of the Manor Court witnessing events in 1732. The case was brought by a Crosthwaite vicar, accusing Newlands farmers and others of defrauding him of tithes due on wool and lambs. On Thursday, 30th March that year, in the dwelling house of Jacob Stamper, innholder, situated in Cockermouth in the county of Cumberland, the witnesses were sworn in and examined. The plaintiff was a Mr. Thomas Christian, BA, who had been vicar of Crosthwaite for about five years, and the accused were Gawin Wren, John Grave, George Hodgson, Joseph Wilson, James Grave, Robert Grave, Peter Wren, Christopher Hodgson, Robert Hodgson and Joseph Fisher. By checking the Parish registers it is possible to discover that these men were farming in a wide area around Keswick: Bassenthwaite, St. John's, Underskiddaw, Ashness, Portinskell and Newlands. Witnesses had been called from all these areas, to be questioned by both sides, so a long session lay ahead!

Representing Newlands and Portinscale were William Dover of Stair and William Dover of Swinside. We do not need here to investigate in detail which branches of the Dover dynasty had produced these two worthies: the continual moving between one farm and another, especially by members of the same families, makes detective work extremely tricky! In the farm at Stair was William the yeoman, aged 38 years. Born in 1694, he had married Jane Fisher in 1715 and by 1732 they had several children. On the last day of March, just into the lambing season, travelling up to Cockermouth some eighteen miles away was probably the last thing William Dover wanted to do! His testimony makes fascinating reading.

Referred to as "the deponent", he states that "by virtue of having been born in the said Parish and living in the said Parish all of his time, he hath been well acquainted with the usages and customs of the said Parish of Crosthwaite in relation to the Payment of the Tythe of Wool there, having had an estate of land at a place called High Snable"(sic). The problem was this; that farmers had been obliged, from time beyond memory, to render to the Vicar a tithe based on one tenth part of the wool sheared from sheep each summer. Although the vicar himself, or his officers, visited each farm to see this wool, it appears that they did not get to see the nine-tenths kept by the farmers, therefore had no way of checking the accuracy of what was being presented to them. As we read William's words we are treated to a first hand account of the sheep farmer's life.

As well as his estate, he had "a considerable stock of sheep of near three hundred, which estate descended to the deponent when he was four years of age", (when his father died). His mother and uncles must have kept things going at High Snab, until William reached sixteen, when he inherited the "herd". Then we come to words that seem familiar: "he kept the said Estate and Sheep until he sold the same about 8 years ago."In the last chapter we learned that, having moved to Portinscale, William had sold the tenancy of High Snab to John Scott in 1722!

Back to the grievances. Although the legal language makes heavy reading, it does give us a sense of the atmosphere in the court, where these down-to-earth, hardy countrymen faced a barrage of formal questions.

"He said that the ancient and usual time of paying and taking the Tythe Wool in the said Parish is and hath been upon the Monday after Midsummer Day yearly, or some few days after, at or near the Respective Dwelling houses of the Parishioners in the said Parish, where the Vicar and his agents or farmers attend. The said Parishioners usually tender and deliver their Tythe Wool by weight (as this deponent did) without the said Vicar or his farmers seeing the nine parts thereof, which is and always was tendered without sight or view, and in such a manner as they think fitt to set out the same as aforesaid".... Then follow details of differences in the value of wool from older sheep and that clipped from the "Hoggs", ie. the one year olds. The going rate was generally 10 pence per hogg except in Borrowdale where it was 11 pence! Furthermore, if lambs are born to Hoggs (by mistake, one assumes, since there are only one or two each year), there was a "modus"to be paid in cash not kind. "The deponent had 2 Hogg lambs which he paid the modus in lieu of the Tythe thereof, and said that John Howe of Latrigg and Daniel Thwaite of Newlands, both of the said Parish, had each of them two Hogg lambs, and this deponent see them pay the modus in lieu of Tythe to Mr. Tullie the vicar at the rate of one halfpenny per lamb."

After this William Dover mentions several other Newlands farmers, including Mr. George Tickell and Mr. Robert Fisher both of "Scalegill", Mr. Francis Ratcliffe of Ullock and Mr. Hugh Tolson of Newlands, "several of them aged and all of them very credible and substantial landholders therin, and kept and do keep very considerable stocks of sheep,"all of whom said that the "modus"was paid for lambs only. The heart of the matter is now examined, and under scrutiny, William has to admit that "in this deponents apprehension the Vicar of the said Parish of Crosthwaite may be defrauded of his just Tythe of Wool in not having the sight of the 9 parts thereof". He even quotes a publicly known case of fraud two or three years previously in Ashness. Finally he has to say that he "verily believes that many of the parishioners (if they be not honest) may impose upon and defraud the Vicar in not letting him have sight of the 9 parts of the Wool".

When William Dover of Swinside ("Gentleman, aged 46") is called to testify, we read much of the same detail in relation to the sheep farming practices. An important piece of information emerges concerning his family background. "Mr. John Dover, his father (remember his will?) kept a stock of sheep of near 300 in number, and this deponent so residing with his father took care of the said flock 'til his father's death about 28 years ago, after which the estate devolved upon this deponent as son and heir, and he purchased his father's said flock of sheep of Susan Dover this deponent's mother.."So far, nothing of note. But a few lines later we read that this father John died when in his 79th year. As this happened twenty eight years before the court case, in 1703, John must have been born in 1625, producing William when he was sixty!

William of Swinside also has to admit that Catherine, wife of John Fisher of Swinside, has told him several times that the clippers were ordered and directed by the Parishioners to "set out and sever the Hogg wool from the rest of the other wool and take out some of the best fleeces", adding that it was common practice.

Not all of the deponents were farmers. James Clark had been summoned from Castle Sowerby because he had been curate to successive vicars in the Parish. His memory went back to Mr. Lowry, vicar from 1667 to 1710, Mr. Tullie, the Dean of Carlisle, at Crosthwaite from 1710 until 1726, and Mr. Nicholson in 1727. In James Clark's opinion the parishioners could and did defraud the vicars of tithes. Others called included some wives and daughters of the defendants, then shepherds and servants.

Finally, Richard Lowry, witness for the plaintiff, with a personal involvement. Son of the vicar in the early 1700s, his testimony struck a note of pathos. It had been well known that the fraud was going on, and Richard himself wanted to fight for justice, but as his father had been too old and sick to pursue the case, "he being of a peaceable temper and having many children to provide for, and the precarious state of his health, and the uncertainty of his life, he thought it most advisable to decline the thoughts of contesting his rights and to take what he could get quietly and peaceably for the sake of his family".

What of the wronged man, Thomas Christian? He had arrived in Crosthwaite in 1727 with his wife and family. In 1730 the registers show that a daughter, Dorothy, was born to Mr. Thomas Christian, Vicar of Crosthwaite, and Dame Elizabeth his wife. In 1731, while the court case must have been looming, another daughter, Mary, arrived. We do not know how many children Dame Elizabeth had borne, her age, or the state of her health, but sadly we learn that in November 1732 she died. It may be that Thomas really needed the extra tithe money to support his family, but even bringing the case could have been very costly. Perhaps it was his nature to pursue wrongdoing fervently. Whatever the case, the vicarage must have been a sad place by the end of the year. The vicar, however, stuck to his case, and in 1734 was still involved in litigation.

From what we have read so far, things seemed stacked against the Graves, Hodgsons, Fishers etc. Sure enough, Thomas Christian won his rights. A little book on the history of Crosthwaite Church, written by Francis Eeles in 1953, provides us with the missing link: he tells of a survey by John Waugh, Chancellor of Carlisle, in about 1749, which states that "Mr. Christian has built a very neat convenient house upon this living. And by a long tedious Lawsuit recovered the right of the Wool as Tything and the Hog wool, which the parishioners would, (and had), covered under a modus for

10d. for every lamb; but he happily prevailed at last, or he had been ruined by it". All seems to have ended well, as Chancellor Waugh reports that "Mr. Christian is regular and exact himself and, notwithstanding the suit, on good terms with them". What we don't know, is how much the proceedings cost the defendants!

By 1740 Thomas Christian had found solace in the arms of another lady, Emma Naylor, who became his wife and produced a daughter in 1742.

William of Stair had also been going through personal griefs at the time of the trial. His wife gave birth to a son, Timothy, in the same year, but he lived only a few months. Higher up the hill, at Swinside too there was sadness at the death of Susan Dover, while in Littletown Edward Jackson's death was promptly followed by those of Ann his daughter and John his son. It is possible that they had been victims of an outbreak of cholera, reported in the Keswick area at that time. Certainly there were many more burials than normal in Crosthwaite during 1731/33. Yet overall in Newlands there was no recorded evidence of the disease. Perhaps the farming people kept well away, as in earlier times. They would have been wise so to do, if we can believe at least half of the conditions described by the historian and writer Hugh Walpole, in his story, "Rogue Herries". Reading his lines does remind us of the constant battle against poverty, filth and illness faced by many in the poorer parts of the towns:

"Keswick, at this time, was a town of one fair street and a huddle of filthy hovels. In the minor streets and "closes"the cottages, little houses and pig-sties were thronged very largely with a foreign and wandering population - riff-raff of every sort who came to steal plumbago from the mines .....these house were crowded with foul middens and encroached on by large open cesspools, pig-sties and cow-sheds. The refuse stagnated and stained the air and tainted the soil. ....At once on entering the town you were in another world far from the honest and independent country of the statesmen and yeomen of the valleys-these statesmen who for centuries had lived on their own land, their own masters, and owned no man anything. In 1731, in Keswick, out of a population of some twelve hundred, nearly five hundred persons had died of smallpox, cholera and black fevers. During the summer months the channels of ordure, the cesspools, became intolerable, and in the lower parts of the town respectable citizens could scarcely breathe."

Other Newlands families too were suffering. John Thwaite and Sarah Wren both died at Littletown, Margaret Clark at Keskadale and George Tickell of Scalegill. Hand in hand with grief, however, in the very same

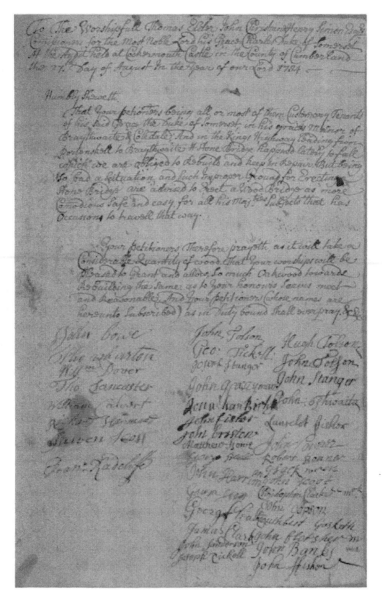

Familiar names, as 38 local farmers sign the plea for help with bridge repairs.

families, went joy, with the celebration of the marriages of Ann Clark of Keskadale, George Scott of Snab, Joseph Fisher and Mary Jackson of Littletown!

With the dawn of the year 1734, while Thomas Christian was relentlessly pursuing offenders, the humble tenants of Braythwaite and Coledale had more pressing problems back in the valley. A petition was sent to the Most Noble Lord, his Grace Charles Duke of Somerset, at the audit held at Cockermouth Castle on the 27th day of August. It is still preserved with the D/Lec. records at the Castle. Interestingly, the Worshipful Comissioners for the Lord included one John Christian, surely a relation.

"Your petitioners being all or most of them Customary Tenants of his said Grace the Duke of Somerset, in His grace's Manor of Braythwaite and Coledale; And in the King's Highway leading from Portenskell to Braythwaite a Stone Bridge happened lately to fall which we are obliged to rebuild and keep in repair. But being so bad a Situation and such Improper Ground for erecting a Stone Bridge, we are advised to erect a Wood Bridge as more Comodious, Safe and easy for all his Majesty's subjects that hao occasion to travel that way.

Your petitioners therefore prayeth, as it will take a considerable Quantity of wood, that your Worships will be pleased to grant and allow so much Oakewood towarde rebuilding the same as to your Honours seems meet and reasonable. And your petitioners (whose names are hereunto subscribed) as in duty bound shall ever pray etc."

Thirty-eight signatures follow the letter. After the neat script of the Petition, the signatures look somewhat ragged and blotchy, but it is a testament to these farmers that many of them could indeed write well. We have met many of them already, and their names come as no surprise. Interestingly, there are no Maysons. A check through parish registers from 1700 until the date of the petition, 1734, reveals a steady decline of survivors in the male line of the family. A John Mayson of Birkrigg did marry in 1713, and on his death in 1739 we learn from his will that he and his wife Mary were still at Birkrigg and had a son Joseph and two daughters An and Francis. Perhaps John's failing health prevented him from taking an active part in the petition. (The Mayson name did live on through at least two more generations of Johns and Josephs).

With this petition there are just a few signs of new blood joining the age-old Newlands community. There were Radcliffes, perhaps related to the wealthy branch of the family in Keswick, Harrimans from Portinscale, and the Jopsons who had moved into to Low House farm and were doing well. In 1728 Edward Jopson,Yeoman, had bequeathed to his beloved wife Dorothy and three daughters Esther, Sarah and Anne, thirty five pounds each as well as one hundred and twenty stone of wool. Twenty pounds and the whole of his flock of 140 sheep went to his son John, whose signature is on the petition, and all the rest of his goods to the two sons Daniel and John. The total value of his inventory, witnessed by Hugh Tolson, John Fisher, John Rawling and William Scott, came to £220.7.10. Perhaps the most significant new arrival is Isack Wren. Branches of the Wren family abounded in the parish of Crosthwaite. It would appear that Isack had recently come into the Newlands area from Piet-Nest near St. John's in the Vale. Born in 1702, he seems to have been extraordinarily unfortunate in his marriages. In 1733, still in Piet-Nest, he married Sarah Jackson, who died, probably in childbirth, the following year, by which time they had moved into Littletown. Two years later Isack married Lydia Gaskarth also of Littletown, but was to bury her after only seven years. Next to take him under her wing was Elinor Fisher, in 1744, and at last the registers show a son and heir John in 1746. Another Wren brother, John, had also settled and married in Newlands, but 1748 was to bring tragedy. In the January John senior died, followed by Isack in the February! The following year at the Court of Dimissions at Cockermouth Castle, where hereditary estates were settled, the Infant John Wren was "admitted"to a tenement in Newlands. His mother Elinor did not re-marry but seems to have done a good job in ensuring the survival of the family. In 1760 her name appears on a list of Enfranchisements, ie. purchasers of the deeds of the farms. "Eleanor Wren of Rogersett, Widow"was buying into the settlement at Birkrigg. Six years later she was also buying property at Littletown from Stephen Fisher. We will be hearing more of him very soon!

With the arrival of families like the Wrens, Radcliffes and Harrimans, and the increase in survival of children in the old-established families, it became increasingly important to maintain and improve property. Several of the petitions to the lord of the manor from around this time reflect the urgent need for timber to restore crumbling buildings, and the difficulty the tenants had in obtaining it. Timothy Fisher declared that his "ancient Barn and Byre is so ruinous and in such decay that your Petitioner, nor his farmers, nor his servants cannot make use thereof for their necessary husbanding". We find John Harriman asking for 5 or 6 trees to repair a barn and stables. John Clark of Keskadell needed "12 trees in the woods belonging to my Lord towards repairing of a fire-house", to which the reply was written "No wood to be granted but upon the tenant's own Estate"! When John Tyson of Stoney-Croft petitioned for wood to rebuild a dwelling house "which had to be taken down because the Miners have driven a level underneath which has shaken the foundations", he was allowed 5 trees, which does not seem very generous. It also reminds us that mining activities were intermittently a part of Newlands life long after the departure of the Germans.

Sometimes the farmers ganged together to give voice to a perceived injustice. An undated document with 30 signatures is addressed to the Right. Hon. George O'Brian, Earl of Egremont and Lord Of the Manor, which puts it between 1750 and 1763. A close study of the men involved narrows it down to around 1755. We read:

"We and our Predecessors have from time Immemorial claimed the timber and other Trees growing in the Hedges of our Customary Estates.....and have Loped them, or cut 'em down for our own Proper Use or Uses without the Stop or Molestation of any Former Lord thereof, or their Agents for the time being. We also think we have an Undoubted Right to Preserve such Trees as we, or our Predecessors have planted, to shelter our houses from the Inclemency of the Weather, and if, by their being overgrown or planted so near our Buildings as to endanger the Walls thereof (which is sometimes the case), we think we have a right to cut them down and convert them to our own proper uses. And likewise...it has been customary for the Tenants to lope the Superfluous Branches of the Lord's Timber trees, or take of the Coppice Woods Growing on such Estates for the purposes aforesaid, without any manner of Stop or Molestation. As these Rights and Privileges were Peaceably enjoyed by the Customary Tenants during the life of His Grace Charles, the Late Duke of Somersett, we are now greatly surprised at the Behaviour of Your Lordship's Agents, and their Deputies in this Country; for they have proceeded against several of Your Lordship's Tenants, (that have cut down or loped Trees growing on their Customary Estates aforesaid). As the Law directs against Persons for cutting down and stealing of Wood, and in Pursuance thereof have obliged them to pay very considerable sums of Money.

If such Prosecution have been carried on by Your Lordship's special advice and direction, (which we hope is not the Case), we flatter ourselves that your Lordship have had our Custom represented in a False Light; We therefore beg leave to give Your Lordship the Trouble of this Remonstrance, hoping on a true Consideration thereof you will please to put a stop to such Rapacious Proceedings in Future, and thereby Prevent us from having recourse to Law (which if possible we chuse to avoid) for the protection of our Custom and Property.

We are, with the Greatest Respect for Yr. Lordship,

Your Lordship's most obedient Tenants....."

Here we have vivid evidence of the troubles besetting the Newlands farmers as they try to get on with life! Not only do they manage the physical demands of tending large flocks of sheep and cattle, the feeding and clothing of their growing families and the provision of safe dwelling houses, but, for what has obviously been a stressful few years, they have been taken to court and fined for using "their own"wood! Again, the names of the petitioners include the old familiar and the new. At the "protest meetings"which must have taken place as they prepared to submit their claim, the Thwaites, Fishers, Scotts and Bonners rubbed shoulders with the Radcliffes, Normans, Fearons and Harrimans.

We end with just one more example of the struggles to co-exist peacefully in the valley. We must admire one Stephen Fisher of Low Snab, who took matters into his own hands, dispensed with the services of a paid Clerk, and, it would appear, wrote his own letter. Records show that he was born in 1732, the son of Joseph and Sarah, and had married Mary Jopson in 1756. Living first at Little Braithwaite, they had buried two young children before successfully raising John, Sarah, Mally, Joseph and Henry. During these years Stephen inherited the dilapidated farmhouse at Low Snab, which was obviously unsuitable for the needs of the growing family. In a clear, but sprawling hand, with much scratching-out and underlining, he addresses Thomas Benson Esquire, Steward and Commisnr. of ye Right Honourable George O'Brian, Earl of Egremont and Lord of the Manor of Braythwaite and Coledale (who had succeeded to the title in 1763). Poor Stephen desperately needs at least fourteen lengths of timber to add to his own, with which he was repairing the ruinous state of Low Snab. Although he has only five oak trees now growing on his estate, he is seeking permission to lop some ash and sycamore from the hedge-row, and twelve firs which he himself planted for house shelter. Having humbly stated his case, Stephen continues: "I am informed by judicious men that all ye aforesaid Wood and Trees will fall half short of what is necessary for repairing and rebuilding"(of Low Snab). Because of this, he also wants to cut down some of the timber on His Lordship's "Wastes". "In the Lane betwixt Dr. Norman's Estate at Stair, and Swinside there is abt. Twenty oak trees most of which are suitable and fit for Timber". It transpires that these trees were formerly part of an estate belonging to a Daniel Fisher of Skelgill, who failed to maintain the Waterbank, about 50 to 60 yds. in length, adjoining the King's Highroad. There were still so many Fishers around the Valley, that it is hard to know exactly what was the relationship between Stephen and Daniel. The petitioner claims that Daniel had possessed the Estate for forty years and upwards, "and have always refused to do anything towards ye repairs of ye sd. Waterbank".

After all his efforts, we learn from a footnote that Stephen was to be allowed 3 of the oak trees and 4 others from the hedgerow, and 6 of his firs! This fell far short of his requirements. However, he and his family did move from Little Braithwaite back into the repaired farmhouse; in 1770 we read of the birth of Robert, son of Stephen Fisher and Mary "of Low Snab", followed two years later by the final confirmation that all had gone well, with the arrival of Mary, daughter of Stephen Fisher of Low Snab, Yeoman.

We have been racing through the eighteenth century, following the little dramas of the Yeomens' lives, with barely a reference to events in the country at large. As always, the mountains around Newlands seem to have cut off the farming community from involvment in momentous changes, even when they took place not many miles away.

Early in the century, James Radcliffe, Earl of Derwentwater, was attainted for high treason and impeached by the House of Parliament for his part in the Jacobite Rising of 1715. Staunch Catholics, the Derwentwaters refused to compromise, at a time when even harbouring priests led to death and disgrace. Rumours must have constantly spread around the Keswick area as well as at Dilston Hall, the family seat of the Radcliffes. So no doubt the farmers did hear some accounts of the terrifying, flaming lights which appeared in the sky following Radcliffe's execution. Indeed, perhaps the children of Newlands gazed in amazement on March 6th 1716, at the wonderful Aurora Borealis which, over in Durham, lit up the hearse carrying Derwentwater's corpse back to Dilston Hall.

A generation later, in 1745, the tradesmen, peddlers and itinerant craftsmen of Cumbria must have brought tales of wars and adventures to the market towns, as Prince Charles Edward Stuart rallied the Scottish clansmen in his attempts to gain the throne. Newsheets carried the news of his victory at Prestonpans and the retreat of Sir John Cope to Berwick. The Young Pretender crossed the Border with five thousand men and marched South, plundering Carlisle, Penrith, Lancaster and Preston. Surely even the Fishers and Dovers wondered what was to happen next! But, by the time the invasion had dwindled down to a dispirited retreat, with the tired Scotsmen retracing their steps, then suffering a catastrophic defeat at Culloden in April 1746, the demands of wintering the flocks and keeping the homesteads warm would again have occupied the farmers' attentions.

It was a era when wars in India, Canada and America were the conversational topics in London and the homes of the landed gentry, when poverty and sickness claimed thousands in the cities, "highwaymen"terrorised travellers up and down the land, and Arkwright and Kay changed the face of industry with the invention of the mechanised spinning-frames. The style of agriculture and the use of the land were also changing throughout England, but those probably the last to be affected by any of this, were our families among the mountains.

By the end of the eighteenth century, up and down the length of England, agriculturalists, educationalists, economists and philanthropists were travelling the newly improved turnpike roads to study the living conditions of townsmen and countrymen alike. How much any number of "-ists"influenced the farmers in Newlands is open to question. In many ways our statesmen bucked the trend. In a time of terrible poverty among agricultural labourers, many of them prospered. While several Acts of Parliament decreed that common land should be enclosed for the promotion of crop growing and control of livestock, the mountainous lands of Cumbria set their own natural boundaries. No local landlords were forcing the yeomen from their family seats in Rogersett. On the contrary any Customary Tenant who could raise the means, had opportunity to "buy-out"his property in a deed of Enfranchisement. The Cockermouth Castle records provide a detailed account of many such negotiations, featuring old-established names, between 1750 and 1800. Just a few of these will show us the progress of these families.

1759 was a particularly busy year for financial transactions. John Cowper, Yeoman, paid £144-0-0 for his two "messuages"at High Snab, with land totalling 60 acres, and an additional £3-14-0 for the right to cut wood. He would still, however, be paying an annual rent to the Earl of Egremont, of £1-1-0. Similarly, we read that George Scott bought tenements at High Snab and Littledale for £190-0-0. Further up the hillside, at Keskadale, a new owner was moving in: John Hudson of Loweswater paid £150-0-0 for a messuage and 70 acres. Some further details from the Indenture, signed and delivered on 1st Dec. 1759, reveal the extremely complicated conditions and clauses which related not only to the farming land, but also very importantly, to all mining rights and future developments.

"For the sum of One Hundred and Fifty Pounds of lawful money of

Great Britain, (and the further sum of One Pound and Six Shillings and sixpence three-farthings for the absolute purchase of the Timber Trees and other Wood and Underwood now growing or which shall hereafter grow upon the said Customary tenements or any Parts thereof, and of the Soil of the Wood and Grounds belonging thereto),..the Lord Egremont doth grant unto the said John Hudson and his Heirs....all those Customary tenements at Newlands called Keskadale". Then follow details of the property and the annual rent of one pound, two shillings and sixpence. The next paragraphs relate specifically to the past history of mineral mining in the valley, with an eye to future possible developments:

"All Mines and Seams of Coal and other Mines and Minerals whatsoever.....and all Quarries of Stone or Slate...for the said Earl etc....at his will and pleasure to search and dig for and work the same..and also the Earth and Rubbish...and (to keep his) Horses, Mares, Geldings and Oxen, Carts, Waggons, Sledges or other Carriages to take, lead and carry away the same,...and to erect Fire-Engines, or other Engines, Stoaths, Smelting houses or any other buildings..Also to make or to lay down any Waggon-ways or other ways and to make any Drains, Cuts or Sluices....Paying a reasonable compensation for the damages".

"John Hudson and his Heirs shall not nor will at any time hereafter, dig for or get any Free Stone, Limestone, Clay, Marl or Slate in or upon the said Premises or any Part thereof, or make any Bricks of the said Clay, except for the purposes of improving the said Enfranchised Premises and repairing the Buildings, Walls and Fences belonging thereto, or erecting new Buildings thereon."

"John Hudson and his Heirs...shall and may for ever hereafter, peaceably and quietly have, hold and enjoy the said Premises hereby enfranchised, and receive and take the Rents, Dues and Profits thereof, without the Lett, Suit, Trouble, Hindrance, Molestation or Disturbance of the said Charles Earl of Egremont etc..."

Enfranchisements in the following years to local men included Stephen Fisher of Low House, Robert Bonner of Portinscale for "Littledale"tenements, Reuben Grave of Skelgill, and John Fisher of Gillbank. An interesting case is that of Eleanor Wren, widow, for Birkrigg tenements: as a widow in 1760,who made only her "mark"on the document rather than a signature - (many of the Newlands men were quite literate by then) - she could have been facing poverty. She was, however, as we have already discovered, the third wife of Isaac Wren, who had bought into

Littletown some thirty years earlier, and after his death in 1748 she had been supported by other members of the family.

However, with other deeds of enfranchisement come signs that "foreigners"were buying in, and some local farmers were struggling to keep their property in the family. So, we read of a Daniel Wilson of Workington, mariner, buying a Littledale tenement, Joseph Dawson of Keswick, a Woodmonger, joining those at Keskadale, and a John Hodgson who was evidently doing alright for himself as an Innholder in Keswick, buying a house at Little Braithwaite, two tenements at Littletown and several small dales "above the beck". In one or two cases, it is quite conceivable that younger generations of some farming families, having left the valley and pursued more lucrative careers, had an interest in buying the properties when the chance arose. Thus we have Mary Scott of the City of London, spinster, buying Mill How tenement in 1778, and William Harryman of the City of London, Gentleman, investing in a dwelling house and two cottages in Portinscale in 1788. Speculation had arrived!

Chapter 8
Travellers and Festivities

At a time when only a few young Cumbrians had a chance to see more of the world outside, many Southerners were "discovering"the North West for themselves. In an age when opportunities for education had led to greater literacy, inquisitiveness and adventure, both men and women ventured into these previously unknown territories, sending back home letters and diaries charged with dramatic descriptions of "horrendous" and "stupendous" mountains. Some visitors came for the express purpose of carrying out a survey, or defining boundaries, while others arrived as "tourists"- the earliest of thousands to follow. Occasionally these intrepid visitors penetrated as far as the Newlands Valley, where their appearance must at times have puzzled the natives.

One of the earliest of all travellers, the intrepid Celia Fiennes, who journeyed through the North on horseback in 1698, had recorded a very

Above: The 'Horrendous Mountains' of Newlands, seen through the eyes of an 18th century painter.

unattractive picture of countrymen's lifestyle: "sad little hutts made up of drye walls, only stones piled together and the roof of same slatts, there seemed to be little or noe tunnels for their chimneys and have no mortar or plaister within or without". Although we know without doubt that the Newlands Yeoman provided a better living than that for his family, there is perhaps a ring of truth in the words of a contributor to "The Gentleman's Magazine"in 1766: many Cumberland farmers "work like slaves; they cannot afford to keep a manservant but husband, wife, sons and daughters all...work in the fields......they very seldom taste meat or wheat bread". Amongst those whose writing gives us an insight into contemporary agricultural conditions, was Arthur Young, who produced his "Six Month Tour through the North of England"in 1770. Around the Penrith area he studied the typical rates for farm labour, including such work as reaping corn, mowing grass, ditching, threshing wheat, barley and oats, and dairy-maids' and young boys' wages.

A more detailed survey was carried out by the Commissioners John Bailey and George Culley in 1794. They found the methods and machinery of Cumberland Statesmen lagging far behind the rest of the country:

"To the small Proprietors, Agriculture, we presume, is little indebted for its advancement: these "statesmen"seem to inherit with the estates of their ancestors their notions of cultivating them, and are almost as much attached to the one as the other: they are rarely aspiring, and seem content with their situation, nor is luxury in any shape an object of their desires; their little estates, which they cultivate with their own hands, produce almost every necessary article of food; and clothing, they in part manufacture themselves; they have a high character for sincerity and honesty; and probably few people enjoy more ease and humble happiness".

Perhaps it does not take too much imagination to weave into this description our own Newlands families. In their section on farm implements, Bailey and Culley see little evidence of modern equipment. A single-horse cart was all that was needed in rough terrain, and they observed such carts being driven by boys and "even women and girls". These were crude, unsafe constructions, with solid cog-wheels and easily displaced axles. We can picture them more clearly with the help of a James Stockdale, who described them many years later: "the revolving axle-trees of the clog-wheeled carts, scantily greased, making each a most unnatural squeak....disagreeable music..about as pleasant as that produced by the "cleaver and marrow bones". (Quoted by William Rollinson in "Life and Tradition in the Lake District"). A vehicle like this could, according to Bailey and Culley, be bought for about

£5 in 1794, but it is more than likely that non-wheeled Sleds were still used by Henry Dover, Reuben Grave and Simeon Thwaite for transporting hay, corn and peat, even by the end of the century.

Winnowing machines had been lately introduced and were now in general use, though "twenty years since, corn was winnowed without any sort of machine; and the farmer was under the necessity of waiting for a natural wind, sufficiently strong to blow the chaff from the grain; and very often had to take it to some eminence at a distance, where the breeze was more certain. Thrashing machines, Drills for Sewing the various kinds of Grain, and Horse-Hoes have not yet found their way into this district".

Their findings also included the information that wheat was grown mainly on the coastal plains, that "bigg", the coarse form of barley with four rows of grain on the ear rather than two, was still by far the most common crop, and that the production of turnips, widely grown throughout the rest of the country, was still largely the practice of the landed gentry. As for peas: "In a climate where so much rain falls, and where the harvest is so precarious, the culture of pease would be attended with so many chances of loss, and so few of gain, that we were not surprised to find them so generally neglected". We can probably assume that peas had not found their way into the "closes"and parcels of land attached to Littletown, Keskadale or High Snab!

High up the valley as these farms were, it is likely that the picture painted by John Housman, in his "Topographical Description of Cumberland, Westmoreland and Lancashire", published in 1800, is pretty close to their pattern of life: "The sheep are kept upon the moors in summer, and frequently in the winter; they are, however, brought down into the inclosures during inclement seasons, when they are fed with hay, which the shepherd carries upon his back to the flocks, sometimes even to the heights of the mountains. Cows are generally kept in the house night and day during winter, except while at water, but some farmers drive them to the pasture where they remain the greatest part of the day. Their common food is the grass of the fields, and hay in the house; and their milk affords great plenty of the finest butter in the kingdom. After taking off the cream, the old milk is either used in the family, sold to those who do not keep cows, at one quart for a halfpenny, or made into cheese, called blue-milk cheese, which is in common use among the country people, as indeed very little of any other sort is made. The butter is either disposed of in the neighbouring market towns, or put up in firkins and sold to dealers, of which it is said, 30,000l worth is sent out of the country annually"

In spite of his analytical mind and keen observation, John Housman occasionally lapsed into a patronising and ridiculously romantic turn of phrase. Thus, he declares of the farmers' daughters: "these healthy-looking maids become alert, hardy and industrious and make excellent wives for men in the same station". And, speaking of those who lived among the mountains, he fantasises: "They, being generally employed in the innocent occupation of tending their bleating flocks upon the hills, and having little commerce with the rest of mankind, till their delightful retreats being discovered, became the objects of admiration to the curious traveller, are modest, unassuming and civil to strangers. This happy people, among whom luxury has scarcely set her foot, and discord is held in contempt, have few wants, and these are moderate and easily supplied"!

It is with this group of "curious travellers"that we find occasional specific references to the Newlands Valley. Celia Fiennes was the precursor of many whose curiosity led them to explore the wild and "horrific"mountains of the Lake District in the eighteenth century. Even though Arthur Young had been concentrating on technical and practical matters, his reports of "Stupendous Mountains"had fired the imaginations of the Romantic writers of the time. Shortly after Young's visit, the clergyman and ex-headmaster, William Gilpin introduced to the English intelligentsia the cult of the "Picturesque", which involved its devotees in a "pursuit"of the beauties of nature. In his excursions around Keswick, Borrowdale, Buttermere and Crummock, it is quite probable that he was one of the first "Artistic men"to observe the day to day lives of our farmholders. Of Newlands he wrote, in 1772, "The mountain valleys we had hitherto seen were rocky, wild and desolate; but here the idea of terror was excluded. The valley of Newlands was even adorned with the beauties of luxuriant nature. We travelled through groves which were sometimes open and sometimes close, with a sparkling stream, the common attendant of these valleys, accompanying us through the whole scene."

Earlier than Gilpin, the poet Thomas Gray had spent a few days in the Lake District, several of them in the Keswick area. His description of an excursion into Borrowdale was written into his "Journal"of 1769, but remained unpublished until 1775, after his death. One of the incidents reminds us of a feature of the dales now sadly missing: "Our farmer was himself the man that last year plundered the eagle's eirie; all the dales are up in arms on such an occasion, for they lose abundance of lambs yearly, not to mention hares, partridge, grouse etc. He was let down from the cliff in ropes to a shelf of rock, on which the nest was built, the people above shouting and hollowing to fright the old birds, which flew screaming round but did not dare attack him. He brought off the eaglet (for there is rarely more than one) and an addled egg……..Seldom a year passes but they take the brood or eggs, and sometimes they shoot one, sometimes the other parent, but the survivor has always found a mate (probably in Ireland), and they breed near the old place".

A few years later, in the erudite and detailed "History and Antiquities of Cumberland and Westmoreland", published in 1777 by Nicolson and Burn, eagles were noted in only four locations: the "Eagle"Crags in Borrowdale, Langdale, Thirlmere and Patterdale. By the end of the century, the children of Borrowdale and Newlands would occasionally see eagles soaring above their fields, but these magnificent birds probably existed more abundantly in romantic poems and legends than in reality. In 1793, the capture of a live eagle in Langdale was rare enough to hit the newspaper headlines.

Nicolson and Burn set out to record, in two great volumes, historical information about every part of the two counties. Their accounts of Newlands centre around the story of the German Miners concluding with their opinion that "these mines, it is said, served not only England, but divers places beyond sea; until the smelting houses and works were destroyed, and most of the miners slain, in the civil wars; and the works have never since been managed to any account". (Only a dozen or so years later, the Dalehead mines were re-opened and new smelting works built in Stoneycroft!) When the writers turned their attention to Keswick they quoted a letter written in 1767 by Dr. John Brown to Lord Lyttleton, and in so doing opened the flood-gates for the surge of Romantic adventurers who wandered the fells for the next fifty years.

In Dr. Brown's eyes, the landscape became a living force, a vividly coloured amphitheatre: "The woods, the grass and the corn fields are nobly contrasted by the grey rocks and the cliffs; and the whole heightened by the yellow streams of light, the purple hues, and misty azure of the mountains. Sometimes the serene air and clear sky disclose the tops of the highest hills: at others, you see the clouds involving their summits, resting on their sides, or descending to their base, and rolling among the vallies as in a vast furnace. When the winds are high, they roar among the cliffs and caverns like peals of thunder; then, too, the clouds are seen in vast bodies sweeping along the hills in gloomy greatness, while the lake joins the tumult, and tosses like a sea."

And so the first wave of tourists came to experience the thrills of Derwentwater: "I will now carry you to the top of a cliff", declares Brown, perhaps on Walla Crag, "where, if you dare approach the edge, a new scene

The view from Swinside, inspiration for Father Thomas West and his Followers.

of astonishment presents itself."And later, a walk in the valley by moonlight "opens a scene of such delicate beauty, repose and solemnity, as exceeds all description".

What, we wonder, did the "content and humble"folk of Newlands make of these misty-eyed visitors, whenever they strayed along the Beck beside their farms. For stray they did. With the publishing of Father Thomas West's "Guide to the Lakes"of 1778, no farmhouse, however hidden in the vale, was safe from prying eyes. In the preface to the second edition of this best-seller, we learn that Father West frequently accompanied "genteel parties"on the tour of The Lakes, and that he made several journeys, on purpose to examine the lakes and to collect information concerning them from the "neighbouring gentlemen". In his words:

"Whoever takes a ride up Newland Vale, will be agreeably surprised with some of the finest solemn pastoral scenes they have yet beheld. Here present themselves an arrangement of vast mountains, entirely new, both in form and colouring of rock; large hollow craters scooped in their bosoms, once the seeming seats of raging liquid fire, though at present overflowing with the purest water, that foams down the craggy brows; other woods ornament their base, and other lakes, clear as the Derwent, lie at their feet.

The softer part of these scenes are verdant hills patched with wood, spotted with rock, and pastured with herds and flocks.

The ride is along Swinside; and having turned the brow of the hill, and passed the first houses, through which the road leads, observe at the gate on the right, a view down a narrow vale, which is pleasing in a high degree. The road continues winding through a glade, along the side of a rapid brook, that tumbles down a stony cannel with water clear as crystal. At the hedgerow tree under Rawlingend (a brawny mountain) turn, and have a new and pleasant view of the vale of Keswick. The road has then a gentle ascent, and the rivulet is heard murmuring below. At the upper end of the cultivated part of the vale, a green pyramidal hill, divided into waving inclosures, looks down the vale upon Keswick. The verdant hills on each side terminate in rude awful mountains, that tower to the skies in a variety of grotesque forms, and on their murky furrowed sides hang many a torrent. Above Keskadale, the last houses in Newland, no traces of human industry appear. All is naked solitude and simple nature. The vale now becomes a dell, the road a path. The lower parts are pastured with a motley herd; the middle tract is assumed by the flocks; the upper regions (to man inaccessible) are abandoned to the birds of Jove. Here, untamed nature holds her reign in solemn silence, amidst the gloom and grandeur of dreary solitude".

Father West then loses himself in a rapturous appreciation of the waterfall on Newlands Hause, below Robinson, "a mountain of purple coloured rock presenting a thousand chasms."And so over to Buttermere, he continues in wondering admiration! That he must have partaken of refreshment and hospitality on his journeys is obvious, though he rarely mentions any individuals. He seems to have been treated well, as he later declares: "If the roads in some places be narrow and difficult, they are at least safe. No villainous banditti haunt the mountains; innocent people live in the dells. Every cottager is narrative of all he knows; and mountain virtue and pastoral hospitality are found at every farm".

Among the many who flocked to view the scenery from West's designated "stations", or viewpoints, turning their backs on the scenery to see it "better"reflected in their Claude Glass, was the young William Wilberforce, on vacation from Cambridge university. One can't help thinking that his observations of the scenery, (including only a fleeting reference to Newlands,) were somewhat more accurate than his pronunciations upon the inhabitants: the Vale of Keswick was "the peaceful retreat of some favor'd Mortals, undisturbed by the Cares and Concerns of the World", and on an after-dinner stroll near Keswick, "a sweet innocent girl directed me the way I should go"!

Perhaps we should pause here, and re-discover the identities of these "Favor'd Mortals", and innocent youths living so happily in such a paradise! Some Coroner's Inquests towards the end of the century soon remind us that life was not always so sweet. For those engaged in any mining activities there was always danger. In September 1768, William Blackstock and William Wilkinson, both probably temporary tenants at Ullock, were killed in a roof-fall, and twenty years later, another mining tragedy claimed the life of an Edward Barren of Braithwaite, this time in the Barrow lead mines. Other Inquests, however, revealed the sadness and pressures of this "idyllic"country life. In October 1788, the cause of Joseph Gill's death was said to be "excessive drinking", a condition which in theory could have claimed the lives of many a hard-drinking valley farmer. Mental illness, or perhaps the pressures of poverty, led one Joseph Fisher of Newlands (but of which branch of the family?) to take his own life in 1776. In the same way, the speculation buzzing around the farms in 1796 would have been on what drove Isaac Fearon to hang himself.

It is unlikely that the old bell-ringers of Crosthwaite Parish church would be very impressed with raptures of the poetic writers. Amongst these men, we read in Nicolson and Burn in 1777, were Mr. Harryman of Portinscale, Mr. J. Bell of Ullock, Mr. John Dover of Spade Forge, Keswick, and Mr. John Fisher, "Lord of Gillbank, Newlands"! (an ancient title carrying more status than wealth!) In one aspect, the opinion expressed by many writers that the "rustic"countrymen did not like antagonism, and on the whole lived peaceably together, may have mirrored reality. We find very few complaints and grievances taken to the Manor courts during this period. In fact, the men of Braithwaite and Cowdale, including Rogersett, quite often just sent a representative to say "All is well". What problems there were, usually concerned blocked waterways or uncleared tracks. In fact, by 1755 and frequently afterwards, we read that "The Turnmen of Rogersett"(ie. those whose turn it was to go to the Court hearings) just didn't bother to turn up! It cost them a fine, but that was no doubt preferable to interrupting work and travelling to Cockermouth for the day. In 1755 the "amercement"was five shillings. In 1759, the inhabitants of Braithwaite, Cowdale and Rogersett failed to send a Turnman to the Court, "for which default we amerce them six shillings and eight pence". By 1796 the fine was ten shillings, by 1807 one pound and one shilling, and by 1817, thirty-nine shillings and eleven pence.

Meanwhile, a new generation of Fishers, Tysons, Gaskarths, Dovers, Graves and Thwaites had been raised in the improved farmhouses of our earlier Petitioners. Problems of repair and maintenance, however, continued to occupy their time. In 1783, William Dixon of Little Baithwaite was requesting six small oak trees from the Lord of the manor to repair the damage done when, "on Friday last, by the overflow of the Water, the Bank of the River burst out and occasioned the Water to overflow all the adjacent ground". Yet again, in 1790, the Fishers, (Daniel this time), needed wood to repair Barn, Byre and Stable at Scalegill.

In 1792, we read of a new name in an old familiar place: "To Thos. Benson Esq., Steward to the Commissioners of the Right Hon. The Earl of Egremont; The Petition of Joseph Pocklington Esq. Herewith......That all his Dwelling House at Stoney Croft and part of the Outhouses being in ruinous condition and very much out of repair, so that they must be taken down and repaired.....Your Petitioner therefore prayeth to have the liberty to cut down Eighteen Oak Trees now growing in his own Grounds at Stoney Croft in order to repair and rebuild the Farms."An ambitious request indeed. But then, Joseph Pocklington was no ordinary man!

During the ten years preceding Pocklington's involvement in Stoney Croft, his fame must have spread even amongst the remote families of Newlands. Thanks to this landed gentleman from Nottinghamshire, and his partner in crime, Peter Crosthwaite, the town of Keswick and the lake beside it had become nationally famous. Following an education at Cambridge and the inheritance of a family legacy, Joseph Pocklington, one-time High Sheriff of Nottingham and bachelor to his dying day, had amused himself in the building of mansions and the creation of his own Coat of Arms. His Lake District visits began in 1768 and continued until, in 1778, he decided to move in, by buying Hestholm, the large island opposite the boat-launch area on Derwentwater. Townsfolk and dalesmen alike must have been eaten up with curiosity as they witnessed the local craftsmen, Samuel Ladyman and his son Thomas, engaged for the next twelve months in transporting across to "Pocklington's Island"the most unlikely array of artefacts. Hidden behind newly-planted Scots pines, gravel paths, a boathouse built to look like a chapel and even a mock church and bell-tower, the new mansion roused local reactions of both amazement and disgust.

Even at this stage, his fame may not have created much stir way out in Newlands. But in August 1781, the young people from the farms must have heard their school-friends in Crosthwaite, or their relatives in the town, talking excitedly of "King Pocky's"latest venture. From the local newspaper of the day we read:

Tuesday August 21st. 1781: "Regatta on Keswick Lake"

The Regatta on the matchless Lake of Keswick will be on the 28th August instant. A prize of Seven Guineas will be given to the winning boat. If more than three boats shall start, the Second shall be entitled to Two Guineas, and the third to One Guinea".

There was also to be a "sweepstake for swimming horses", an idea copied, as was the whole venture, from a previous regatta on Bassenthwaite Lake.

Back in Newlands, twenty-one year old Mary Fisher, daughter of John and Grace at Swinside, with her cousin Mally, Henry Tyson from Stoneycroft and perhaps another youngster of the Fisher clan, Timothy, son of Joseph and Mary at Birkrigg, could well have set out in eager anticipation of some unusual events. On that day, however, their spirits as well as their clothes were no doubt quashed by the most horrendous downpour seen in the Keswick area in many years. The "Cumberland Pacquet"reported that the planned mock attack on the Island by the assembled fleet had to be postponed until night-time. Any young folk who had set out hopefully from Newlands that morning must have arrived home in a pretty sorry state.

In the August of the following year, however, the sun shone on the appointed day. If the report in the Cumberland Pacquet on that occasion is to be believed, it would have been impossible for the young folk of Swinside, Littletown, Low Snab or Skellgill not to know what was happening.

"At eight o.clock in the morning, a vast concourse of ladies and gentlemen appeared on the side of the Derwent Lake, where a number of marquees, extending about 400 yards, were erected for their accommodation."

As the races began, crowds lined not only the lakeshore but every hillside: "A view from any of the attendants boats (of which there were several) presented a scene which beggars all description. The sides of the hoary mountains were clad with spectators, and the glassy surface of the Lake was variegated with a number of pleasure barges, which, tricked out in all the gayest colours and glittering in the rays of a meridian sun, gave a new appearance to the celebrated beauties of this matchless vale."

Surely somewhere up on Yewthwaite Hause, twixt Catbells and Maiden Moor, sat the eighteen year olds, Joseph and Martha Fisher, Agnes Tyson and Daniel Dover? They would have witnessed the enemy fleets advancing from behind Friar's Crag and forming into a curved line, then heard the "terrible cannonade, accompanied with a dreadful discharge of musquetry...This continued for some time, and being echoed from hill to hill, in an amazing variety of sounds, filled the ear with whatever could produce astonishment and awe. All nature seemed to be in an uproar..."

With the fall of evening came fireworks and a ball. Perhaps the latter was beyond the aspirations of humble farm folk, but as this Regatta became an annual event, sooner or later some ambitious young farmer's son may have found his way into higher circles. Ending his own report of the Regatta, the writer John Housman stated, in 1800, that "lately that sort of diversion has been discontinued, not being suitable to the rural simplicity of these peaceful and sequestered vales". (It sounds almost as though the "Friends of the Lake District", or the National Park Authority had put in an early appearance, whereas in fact the two driving forces behind the great project, Pocklington and Crosthwaite, had experienced some dismal failures in later events and had run out of ideas!)

Pocklington had, by this time, shown an interest in several large properties in the area, extending, rebuilding and transforming as he went. As he died a bachelor, it is unclear what happened to Stoneycroft after his request for rights to rebuild in 1792. But we must assume some family continuation there, because, half a century later, we can follow a complicated series of agreements between a Revd. Roger Pocklington of Ollerton in the County of Nottingham, and several others, leading to his Purchase of the Enfranchisement of Stoney Croft in 1857.

Having tried to imagine some of the grander diversions of the 1780s, we could also look at the more frequent ways in which the local youth met to have fun. Reading the brilliantly vivid account of these by John Housman, whose "Topographical Description"we have already quoted, transports us into the midst of the revelries which no doubt characterised a Keswick "night out":

"In their dances, which are jigs and reels, they attend to exertion and agility more than ease and grace; minuets and country dances constitute no part of these rural assemblies. Indeed, their dancing parties often exhibit scenes very indelicate and unpleasant to the peaceful spectator. No order is observed, and the anxiety for dancing is great; one couple can only dance their jig at the same time, and perhaps half a dozen couples stand on the floor waiting for their turns; the young men, busied in paying addresses to their partners, and probably half intoxicated, forget who ought to dance next; a dispute arises; the fiddler offers his mediation in vain; nay, the interference of an angel would have been spurned at: blood and fury! It must be decided by a fight, which immediately ensues. During these combats, the whole assembly is in an uproar; the weaker part of the company, as well as the minstrels, get upon the benches, or stand in the corners, while the rest support the combatants, and deal blows pretty freely among each other; even the ladies will not infrequently fight like Amazons in support of their brothers, sweethearts or friends. At length the fight is over, and the bloody-nosed pugilists and unfeathered nymphs retire to wash and readjust their tattered garments: fresh company comes in, all is quiet again and the dance goes on as before; while the former guests disperse into different public houses, and the recounter, which generally commences without any previous malice, is rarely again remebered".

Perhaps our farmstead youngsters did not often have the chance to travel into town for such merriment, but on certain key occasions in the farming year, there would be plenty of excuse for feasting and dancing nearer home. At Christmas, Easter, Whitsuntide, the end of sheep-shearing, and harvest-time, families would get together for mutual help followed by celebrations. And twice a year, many would witness, or participate in, the "Hiring"Fairs, at Whitsuntide and Martinmas. Held locally at Cockermouth, these were the occasions on which young labourers, servants and maids, would find employment to see them through six or twelve months with a local farmer. In the market place, in the midst of farmers selling livestock, potters selling their wares, travellers with materials, ribbons and magic potions, all those offering themselves for employment would stand around with a piece of straw or green branch in their mouths, ready to catch the eye of a potential employer. The day would always end in festivities and dancing, probably just like Housman's description!

We can bring the century to a close with a first-hand account of a walk in the Newlands valley. Captain Joseph Budworth arrived in the Lakes for "A Fortnight's Ramble"in 1795. In a chatty sort of way he describes what he sees without resorting to the overblown hyperbole of his predecessors. Chapter 8 of his book takes us into Newlands.

"We passed along the Cockermouth road for a mile and a half; then turned towards Newland valley, keeping a most enchanting sight of Bassenthwaite Lake, and frequently of Derwentwater, Keswick appearing to the best advantage it can be seen in. Instead of keeping to the road, we dropped down some fine pastures, until we came to a deep brook. The bridge had been carried away, a victim to the floods, which obliged us to go higher than the point we intended making; however, we found a ladder some good-natured farmer had laid across for general accommodation.

Before we reached the brook, we saw a treble-trunked oak; the centre trunk was hollow, and a mountain-ash grew out of it; about two yards down it we broke a hole with our sticks, and the ash was strong and healthy.

We now reached the side of the hill; and being at a loss which way to proceed, an old woman upwards of ninety, who was keeping house whilst the family were at harvest, directed us to the head of Newland, where we stopped at a large farmhouse, and asked for some whey. They had two machines at work (each of which could churn thirty pounds), and were making butter for salting. In an instant we had two bowls of whey, and half a dozen hands offered us chairs. We were pleased in thinking every trifle interesting that so agreeably proves the active civility of these mountaineers: and who would not?"

Over two hundred years later, hospitality in the shape of cups of tea and cakes is still offered to the weary traveller at Low Snab farm, high in the Vale.

Chapter 9
Newlands Chapel

"Newlands chapel, about four miles from the mother church, hath an ancient salary of 2l. 12s 0d, and hath thrice received 200l by lot, viz. In 1748, 1750 and 1757, with which sums lands were purchased in the chapelry of Loweswater and in the parish of Crosthwaite, of the present yearly value of about 22l". Words from the Nicolson and Burn History in 1777.

Through all the centuries of our Newlands journey so far, a simple stone building, the chapel, has stood hidden by trees in the very heart of the community. Nowadays a handful of people carry on the age-old tradition of worship there, and many other visitors spend a few moments of their holiday in quiet meditation, or just appreciation of the tranquillity. Most of the families we have been following will, at some stage or other, have been involved in the worship or the management of this ancient house of God.

Newlands chapel is mentioned again in the most detailed of all the

Above: Newlands Church, the hub of life in the valley for six centuries.

"Histories"at the end of the eighteenth century. William Hutchinson's two-volume work of 1797, covered both Cumberland and Westmorland. He found the town of Keswick disappointing, with most of the houses low and meanly built, but like all others before him, he fell heavily for the charms of Newlands; "this is a most pastoral scene - little cottages were seen dispersed among the hedgerow trees, and cattle and sheep, depasturing, climbed the steeps".

Hutchinson also gives information from the Crosthwaite parish registers, and includes the information that, in 1790, "they had begun to baptize at the chapels of ease - 48 were baptized at the mother church (St. Kentigern's), - at Borrowdale chapel 12, Newlands 5, Thornthwaite 9, St. John's 13 and at Wythburn 5, - total 92."It is time to take a look at the little chapel in the heart of the valley. We jump way back to the sixteenth century.

In 1559 Archbishop Parker had written that the "Order for serving Cures is now destitute". When he was writing, many of the remote chapels in the dales were without an "incumbent", a qualified member of the clergy. Such chapels must have been in existence for many, many years by then. Deprivation, death and sickness had taken their toll, especially in the plague of 1558. It was decreed that "readers"could be appointed in places of need, who could literally read the service, but were not allowed to christen infants, take marriage services, or even communion. The principal pastor of the area had to see to these as he made a circuit of the parishes. A further comment on the situation came from Chancellor Ferguson of Carlisle, in his Diocesan History of the area. He described many large parishes with "inadequate stipends": "The sole endowment of these chapelries was a few shillings, which the inhabitants had, at some remote period, agreed to charge upon their estates", (hence the "bequests"in the 17th century wills that we will look at.)

In Keswick, an ecclesiastical Commission was set up in 1571 to regulate the management and religious practices of the church at Crosthwaite. A body of 18 "Sworn Men"was given strictly detailed instructions on the order of divine services, the books to be used, the administration of the sacrament, and the governing body of the school. Reference was made in this Commission to the nearby chapels "thereunto belonging", amongst which was Newlands. The Bishops granted the licences for these chapels, usually for a sum of about £4, which would be raised by the local people, who were bound by deed. The money would be raised through a rate on land, or by a charge for seats in the chapel. As this seems to have been a well-established practice since the mid-fourteen hundreds, we can reasonably assume that there was a chapel in Newlands serving the needs of those farms and families we met in chapter one! With the publication of an early map of Cumberland, we have the proof we need. However inaccurate these early maps might have been with regard to roads, lakes and towns, the cartographers usually managed to pop the little symbols for places of worship into the right slots! So, in Saxton's map of Cumberland, dated 1576, we find a chapel in Newlands. Some years later the house of worship is marked again, on the 1610 map by John Speed.

When we think of the rough and rude construction of sixteenth century farm-houses, it is hard to imagine that an early place of worship in Newlands would be much more than a rough stone building with a thatched roof. It is likely that a small tax was levied on either property or animals, towards the building and costs of keeping the place of worship dry and safe. In an early manor-court roll, from 1523, was a reference to an "Ox tax, for the building of the church of Crosthwaite". Although there probably weren't many oxen in Rogersett, no doubt some relevant scheme was employed. We have John Mayson of Stoneycrofte to thank for our first real link between the building and the local people. In his will, 1594, he bequeathed to Newlandes Chappell the sum of 3s.4d. Two years later, the deceased John Thwaite was declared to be owing the Chapel two sums, of £1-18-4, and £1-1-11. The will of John Dickinson of Bodehole (Bawd Hall) in 1612 also records a sum to be given to the Chapel, but there are very few other specific bequests after this. Perhaps the parishioners felt that whatever tax had been already levied upon them was quite enough!

We have come now to the times when more detailed records are available. In the year 1616, the parishioners of Crosthwaite, and especially of Newlands, witnessed a dramatic set-to between the clergy and the 18 Sworn Men. (For the details of this I am indebted to Mr. Tom Wilson's fascinating little book, "The History and Chronicles of Crosthwaite Old School", 1949.) The Vicar of Crosthwaite, Giles Robinson, had crossed swords with the worthy band of 18 parishioners over several matters and had taken it upon himself to put 13 of them in jail! One of the issues involved the schoolmaster, James Garth, who also happened to be the Curate of Newlands Chapel. The sworn men had declared that Garth was guilty of "gross offences and negligences", and had given him notice to depart. Garth, aided and abetted by Giles Robinson and his brother Henry, none other than the Lord Bishop of Carlisle, had refused to comply.

At this time in Newlands there was a population boom. Not only would the Maysons, Bonners, Dovers and all the others meet James Garth at chapel on Sundays, but also the news of the school dispute would be brought into the valley through the many children who made the daily treck to learn reading and writing. The oldest among them, probably the thirteen year- olds John Mayson and Elizabeth Dover, along with Robert and Hugh Mayson, Hugh Rawling and Katherine Clark, would be responsible for the safety of the young ones, Agnes Fisher or Elizabeth Towlson, aged only eight.

Back in Keswick an inquiry was held. The town would be alight with curiosity and gossip as, on 16th of February, 1616, a body of high officials rode in to hear the witnesses. A jury of laymen was appointed, and eventually the verdict was given against the Vicar and the Bishop, and the 13 men were released from jail. We do not know whether James Garth was allowed to continue as Curate in Newlands for much longer! It is doubtful, as we very soon read of a successor. In chapter 4 we came across the burial records of Sir Christopher Scott, Curate of Newlands, and his wife Elizabeth, during the years of sickness, 1621-3.

A succession of fairly short-term appointments saw the Chapel through the years 1630 to 1700. During this time, curates or readers had to steer their flock through the turmoils of the Civil Wars, the Commonwealth with its change in the laws governing church worship, the establishment of Justices of the Peace to conduct marriages and funerals, and the burgeoning Quaker movement. Anthony Bragg, James Grave, Simon Atkinson, Gawin Gibson and Thomas Birkhead were very likely local men, educated at Keswick Free school, then remaining in their local community to work in the church. To quote W.G. Collingwood, in his "Lake District History", "In the little chapels… it was usual for the incumbent to teach school, sometimes to the scandal of the authorities who found the communion table inked and so forth". Perhaps the younger Newlands children were taught by Thomas Birkhead, who in 1678, married Hana Shepard, was appointed Curate at Newlands, and had the joy of seeing his son Thomas baptised! An interesting year for the valley!

The year 1703 saw a comprehensive study of the diocese undertaken by a dedicated Bishop, William Nicolson. In his comments on Crosthwaite, he included details of the endowments of the five Chapels of Ease. Of these, Thornthwaite was the most well cared for, whereas Newlands came below Borrowdale, St. John's and Wythburn, with a salary of just £2.15s.1d. He then adds an interesting comment, although it is hard to know how well it applied to Newlands: "As mean as these salaries look, the Readers in these dales are commonly more rich than the Curates (much better provided for in appearance) in other parts of the diocese; having the Advantage of drawing Bills, Bonds, Conveyances, Wills, etc. which the Attornies elsewhere claim as their property: but since the Duty of stamp'd paper came in Fashion, their Revenues are much abated on this Article".

At the time of Bishop Nicolson's report, a John Atkinson was Curate in Newlands. Appointed to the position in 1690, John had obviously settled well into the valley and stayed far longer than some. In 1708 he married Catherine Bonner of Littletown, from a family living there since the 1500s. They raised a large family, and John served the community until 1728. After a couple of short-term appointments, a worthy successor was found. In 1731, Joseph Fisher became Reader, but some years later gained the title of Curate without any special training for the job!

According to Nicholson and Burn in 1777, he was licensed in 1731, the same year in which he married his wife Sarah. Joseph came from the long-established Fisher families of Newlands, and initially, despite perhaps a superior education, his standing was very much that of other local men. According to Bouch and Jones, ("The Lake Counties, 1500 to 1830"), the readers about that time, "in some poor and remote chapelries, were perhaps the only factor preserving the people from heathendom". Their very small salaries were augmented by "whittlegate"and "harden sack". The former referred to the custom that the reader would be given food, and board if necessary, at several different farms in the area, and would take with him his own "whittle"ie: knife, as very few hosts would have spare implements. The harden sack, or "hempen sark", was a supply of suitable clothing for his position. Possibly Joseph, living at Littletown, did not need to recourse to such help, but even so, an event of 1748 must have been music to his ears. It had been decreed by Queen Anne, in 1704, that a charity should be established whereby the "first fruits and tenths"of the revenue of the church should be set aside for income for the poorer parish livings. The strange thing was, that this should be administered by lot, resulting in a somewhat unfair distribution. Newlands chapel, however, had the good fortune to receive no fewer than three awards of £200, in 1748, 1750 and 1757. At the same time, changes were made under George II, which meant that any Chapelry receiving augmentation from "Queen Anne's Bounty"would automatically become a Perpetual Curacy, with priests rather than readers. As it would have been less than humane to eject the existing readers, they were transformed overnight, without any examination, into ordained priests. So it was that

Newlands, after its good fortune of 1748, became a Parish. Joseph Fisher, who in 1745 when his daughter Dinah was baptised, was "Reader at Newlands Chapel"(as well as headmaster at the Keswick school), became an ordained Deacon in 1749. Now that Newlands was Parochial, there was an added obligation on the parishioners to contribute to the Curate's salary and to maintain the church fabric. The burden was eased by the fact that, after three awards from Queen Anne's Bounty, lands were purchased in the Chapelry of Loweswater, bringing in a small revenue. Almost a hundred years later, the eminent Keswick resident, Robert Southey, drawing no doubt on local legend and hearsay, referred to Joseph Fisher, and shed light on his still frugal existence: "The person who was thus Reader, as it was called, at yonder Chapel in the Vale of Newlands, and who received this kind of ordination, exersised the various trades of Taylor, Clogger and Butter-Print maker"(Colloquies. Vol II).

It is still possible, however, that Joseph Fisher was in a position to help his parishioners financially: although we do not know how and if he was involved personally, it is recorded in Nicholson and Burn that "in his time the Chapel was rebuilt". A final indication of his comparative wealth comes in an Indenture of 1774. At the end of a fruitful and useful life, Joseph Fisher died in 1779.

There was slight hiccup in the smooth running of Chapel affairs in 1764. Mr. John Harrison had succeeded Joseph Fisher, not only as Curate but also as master at Keswick School. Some of the trustees felt that he was not giving enough time and energy to his pupils, and forced a vote. Harrison held on to his post by just one vote, that of the Vicar. But his opponents canvassed the support of the following year's trustees, and the schoolmaster -cum-Curate survived only one more term of office. The legal Bond drawn up to settle the case can be seen in the Keswick Museum.

From 1794 until 1826 the Rev. William Parsable was Curate of Newlands as well as headmaster of the Free School. Mr. Tom Wilson gives us a vivid account of an incident in 1801:

"The Reverend gentleman was a strict disciplinarian, and was rather crotchety. It is probable that at that time everyone was a bit on edge. Napoleon Bonaparte was at Bologne with a very big army, waiting to cross the Channel to invade our shores.

News was scarce, rumour rampant, the local Volunteers drilled and manoeuvred at Spooney Green, affording other interests than lessons at school. Negligence of the scholars together with absenteeism, played considerably on the master's nerves, and on occasions he gave way to violence, much to the discomfort of the scholars and the annoyance of their parents. Complaints were made to the Sworn Men, but "Peppery Billy"went his own way, until "the Trustees were as flayte of him as were the scholars". William Slack, a wealthy man now resident at Monk Hall, was interested. He had a nephew and a niece attending the school from "Lissick"Hall. The little niece was not slow to tell her uncle how her brother had been well and truly flogged. William worked himself into a rage and went to the school to seek some explanation, and after an altercation with the master, took him by the neck and the pants, and in front of the scholars, put him out of the school. Outside, the fracas continued, with en excited and interesting audience in attendance".

Imagine the chatter...the "crack"...in Swinside, Littletown and Birkrigg that evening. With no phones for checking the details amongst each other, mums and dads would be hurrying across fields and down lanes to find out just what their priest had been up to! Peter Wren, Moses Mawson, Henry Dover and several others would be hearing again and again the dramatic accounts from their excited, or perhaps frightened, children. Inevitably, there was a prolonged follow-up of the incident, resulting in a court case in Lancaster. It must have been very hard for parishioners to concentrate on whatever message the Reverend Parsable was trying to deliver to them on Sunday mornings. In the end, William Slack was fined £200, but was given a hero's welcome back in Keswick!

From existing chapel records we know that things must have settled down, as Mr. Parsable continued as Curate in Newlands until 1826. It is at this stage that we are fortunate enough to have detailed copies of the Chapel Wardens' "Book of Accompts", and can follow various activities and developments in chapel life.

In 1808, when records had just been started in the book, a comprehensive list was drawn up of every tenement in Newlands, with "Ancient Owners", (those whose names the tenements still were known by), "Present Owners", and "Occupiers", the latter distinction giving us a clearer picture of which families were still prospering and which seemed to be fading. There were 32 tenements, and these were divided into groups of 4 for the purposes of drawing up a rota of Chapel Wardens. A typical group would be: "Cowpers/Ekin/Thwaite's/ Birkrigg". Most of the names are very familiar, but creeping in amongst the Present Owners are some newcomers, whose stories we will look at later. What we do learn from these early accounts, is that every year four new Chapel wardens were appointed, and were entrusted with a capital sum of £18, "equally divided for which they are to pay interest at the rate of 5% per. annum to the Curate at Martinmas next". Hardly high finance! For the next few years there are no other details of chapel affairs, but from the rota of wardens we can see who were the trustworthy and respected farmers. While mighty battles were fought on land and at sea between warring European countries, England celebrated victory at Waterloo, and cities up and down the country buzzed with news of Bonaparte and Nelson, the Chapel Accompts book faithfully records that the Graves, Wrens and Mawsons were estaWe come to the year 1824, when the wind of change began to stir some age-old customs. The Rev. William Parsable, still Curate, and seven worthy parishioners, held a Vestry meeting when it was agreed that the "Chapel Stock", or "Lenten Stock", namely the £18 which had been passed down in keeping of the Churchwardens for many generations, would be totally held by the Curate, who would be satisfied with whatever interest he could make from it with his own investments He bound himself to refund it at any given notice, and agreed that the surety note, for any refunding, would be kept by Mr. Peter Wren, Snr. of Littletown. Future Vestry meetings were to be held at Whitsuntide rather than Martinmas "on account of the lateness and often inclemency of the season". The other change was that instead of four, there would be only two Chapelwardens each year.

The following year the Chapelwardens rota was revised, featuring a newcomer, John Walker, among the owners, and Wilson Tyson as the occupier at Mill Dam. Other families had passed their duties on from father to son. By 1826 a new Curate had arrived to take Mr. Parsable's place. James Currie seems to have inherited a crumbling edifice, as it is from this time, over the next few years, that we read of various attempts to patch up the chapel. Thus in 1832 the accounts included "to cash paid for repairs and expenses £1. 14. 4"followed in1834 by "to John Lancaster for repairing Chapel £0. 11. 02". Each set of figures also included a mysterious "Journey to Wigton"by one of the Wardens, perhaps to buy new books of "Articles"or to present the accounts. In 1837 an interesting item of expense throws light on the schooling of the younger children: "to Robert Dixon for new school tables £1. 2. 2."which he had provided along with new leaded light and three squares of glass for 4s. 4d.

By 1837 a crisis was looming. The costs of all the repairs had overtaken any income, so it was agreed that a rate of 2d in the pound should be collected in place of the old 1/2d. In this way a grand total of £3. 15. 11.

came into the coffers, but was very soon to be swallowed up in major works. For two years the wardens struggled to meet the costs of new locks, keys, nails, linen, a new "Bason for Baptisms"and even 1s.0d "to keep the roof clear of drops".

There were two separate issues urgently needing attention, and in 1841, in a major upheaval, both were rectified.

"In the year of our Lord one thousand eight hundred and forty one a School-House was erected at the West end of Newlands Chapel. The expense of the workmanship and materials was defrayed by subscription, but all the materials were conveyed to the place by the inhabitants of Newlands at their own expense. (Rev. John Monkhouse, Perpetual Curate, John Wood, John Dover, Chapel Wardens.")

After a list of Subscribers, we read another memorandum:

"The Chapel of Newlands, being in a dilapidated condition, requiring a new Roof, Windows and end Wall besides other sustatntial repairs, and there being no convenient place for the administration of the Holy Communion, it was considered necessary that the walls should be raised in order that a Gallery might be erected for the purpose of obtaining this desirable accommodation, and a few free sittings, the expense of which defrayed by subscription. The Font was given by William Denton Esq. and the Chalice by Arthur E. Hulton Esq."

The Rev. John Monkhouse had succeeded James Currie in 1840. He was a man of considerable wealth, and no doubt powerful means of persuasion amongst would-be Subscribers to his cause. To John Dover, John Wood, Moses Mawson and all the other Wardens worshipping week after week in the leaking, draughty Chapel, he must indeed have been a gift from God, a second "Gots Gabt"for Newlands.

In the first group of Subscribers, those who contributed to the building of the school, John Monkhouse sets the course with £10. In first place on the second list, that for Subscribers to the new Chapel, is none other that "Her Majesty the Queen Dowager"with exactly the same amount! The school benefited from many well-known local Gentry. The Speddings of Mirehouse, Sir John Woodford, General Wyndham in Cockermouth and the Hon. J R Curzon from Portinscale all managed a pound or two. At the other end of the scale, some Newlands families also dug deep in to their pockets to give seven, five or even just two shillings, to ensure a place of education for their children. The total cost was £37. 0. 6.

The Chapel, however, needed a lot more money. The task of rallying support was no doubt taken on chiefly by the Curate, but many Crosthwaite people were employed in supplying, carting, or building with, locally available materials. A Mr. Walker charged £4 for drawing up the Plans, Hodgson and Gibson, the chief builders, claimed £52. 10, Powley the Joiner wanted £64. 6. 0, and Christopherson, a Keswick man, put together a bill of "about"£31. 14. 5(!) for a variety of items such as Paint and Varnish, Cloth for Stools and Oil for Seats. Materials including Glass, Wood for Glazing Windows, Stone Flags from Quay Foot, and Bells, all contributed to the total expenses of £200. 3. 0. A reminder of the need for heat in the building comes as we read of "Poker and Tongs"costing 3/9d, and finally Mary Fisher was given the task of cleaning the chapel and paid 5/-.

The inhabitants of Newlands had themselves contributed £32.0.0. to this massive project. The Rev. Monkhouse came up with another £77.0.0, and the Speddings and Stangers combined raised £30. A Mrs. Peachy on Derwent Isle gave £3.0.0. She was the widow of Colonel Peachy who had bought the Island from Joseph Pocklington. Other local clergy played their part, with £2.2.0. from the Vicar of the new St. John's church in Keswick, £2.0.0. each from the Revs. Edward Wilson and D. Hunter of Crosthwaite, and £2.0.0. from a Rev. Wm. Monkhouse of Goldington, surely a relative of John in Newlands. Finally, among the dozens of names of well-wishers sending small amounts, we find the humble "A friend"parting with £1.0.0. In all, £200. 3. 0. was subscribed, and was neatly accounted for during the next two years.

All of this work must have been going on during 1842/3; children growing up around it; farmers carrying on the annual tasks of harvesting and lambing; the ceremonials for births, marriages and deaths somehow continuing; the weather no doubt atrocious at times, hindering the progress. What joy there must have been when all workmen finally departed and the people of Newlands could gather again in their "new"ancient place of worship.

The regular Chapelwardens' Accounts resume in '44, with Thomas Hodgson, Farmer of Littletown, and Isaac Gill for High Tenement continuing the duties, and Mary Fisher still cleaning the Chapel for 5/-. In the next few years, Reuben Dover supplied peat, presumably for a fire to heat the Chapel, a new Bell-Rope was purchased for 6d. and the Curate was treated to a new linen Surplice for £1. 3. 4.

From about this time, we find a plan of "Chapel Sittings"in the new Church, which probably meant a fee charged for the privilege of having a family pew. (We remember that "a few free sittings"were to be a feature of the re-construction). Several families were thus represented:

Communion Table

| Reading Desk | | Pulpit |
| Parsonage | Font | |

| 2 Keskadale: Fisher | 2 Littletown: Nicholson |
| 1 Low Houses: Clark | 1 Gillbrow: Gordon |

3 Birkrigg: Gibson	1 Aikin: Grave
	1 Bodehole: Harrison
	1 Littletown: Sleap

1 Emerald: Mawson	3 Littletown: Wren
1 Parsonage	
1High: Hewson	

| 2 Lowhouse: Thwaite | 1 East House: Threlkeld |
| 1 High Snab: Lawson | 2 High Snab: Davis |

| 2 Gill Bank: Harriman | 3 Low Snab; Mawson |
| 1 Mill Dam: Edgar | |

It is noticeable that by the 1840s many properties had come under new ownership by "offcomers", people quite new to the Valley. How they fared, we will look at in a later chapter. In the meantime, only ten years after the upheaval of the re-building, the structure of the house of worship was again causing concern. Yet again, the Rev. John Monkhouse came to the rescue:

"At a Vestry Meeting held this day, Jan.2nd 1851, duly and lawfully called, it was decided by those whose signatures are below, that the South wall of the Chapel be pulled down and rebuilt. The inhabitants of Newlands agreeing to lead all the materials necessary and the Rev. John Monkhouse agreeing to subscribe half the expense of rebuilding".

John Monkhouse, Perpetual Curate, Moses Dover and John Dover Chapelwdns.

Jos. Wren Peter Wren	John Herd	
John Clark	Thomas Hodgson	John Bowness
Daniel Thwaite	Isaac Gill(X his mark)	
Fisher Thwaite.		

At the same meeting it was decided that the eighteen pounds which for years had been held in trust, was to be used to drain the estate at Fangs in Loweswater, with John Monkhouse subscribing £32 for the same purpose. "The Living will thereby receive at the least six pounds in the year".

William Hodgson, Mason, of Applethwaite, agreed to pull down the South wall of the Chapel and rebuild it, laying the stones outside in Roman Cement and putting in Tabling every three feet. He agreed to "build it in a workmanlike manner and to plaster it, for the sum of Eighteen Pounds. (A Note) Rebuild in June."

Now halfway through the nineteenth century, we will leave the Chapel celebrating one more important event.

It is Christmas Day, 1856. Busy parents and excited children have made their way to the Chapel, where an elderly gentleman from Skelgill is joining the celebrations, as he has done for over seventy years. Today, John Fisher Esq. sits at the front as the Revd. Monkhouse addresses him:

"We, the inhabitants of Newlands beg to express to you our grateful acknowledgement of your munificence in presenting the handsome sum of £100 to the uses of the Sunday School of this Place.

We are duly sensible of the great benefits which arise from such a system of awards as it is your object to perpetuate, and we hope that neither our children nor our childrens' children may ever forget by whose bounty they are indebted for the advantages which will be secured to them."

Some months earlier, we learn from the Book of Accompts, Joseph Fisher had applied to the Charities Commissioners for authority to set up a trust fund for the Chapel, with a donation of £100 to be invested, and the interest of £3 per annum to be used as the Trustees thought fit. The commissioners, however, stipulated that some specific use must be made of the £3. It was decided that with this money "Bibles, Prayer Books, and other Religious Books, published by the Society for the promotion of Christian Knowledge should be given as rewards to the Children attending the Sunday School at present established in the Chapelry of Newlands"".

The Sunday school at the time must have been bursting at the seams, as the Baptismal records for the previous ten years show a population boom among the Mawsons, Fishers, Hodgsons, Gaskarths and other farming families. The congregation included John Jackson the schoolmaster, and the families of Wilson Tyson a slate-quarry worker, and Henry Lowden the Innkeeper at Mill Dam. We leave the celebrations at this point to look at the changing face of Valley life over these past few decades.

Chapter 10
Innkeepers and Miners

The last person mentioned in chapter 9 was Henry Lowden, "Innkeeper", at Mill Dam. In the early years of the nineteenth century, the flow of tourists to the Lakes gave rise to an increase of Inns and Public Houses, not only in the towns, but in the surrounding "picturesque" areas. As artists and writers ventured further and further from the recognised "viewing stations"in search of their own experience of mountain solitude, valley-dwellers in Newlands must have become accustomed to the sight of strangers staring in at their windows, scrambling up the sides of waterfalls, and watching the gathering of the flocks.

Such an adventurer was Samuel Taylor Coleridge, poet and friend of Robert Southey at Greta Hall. In September 1800 he described one of his solitary excursions in his notebooks. He had walked around the hillsides to Swinside, and from there looked out over the Vale of Newlands, "so arborous as to look almost like a Somersetshire Vale; the winding river with its arched bridges....I went down the lane, crossed the bridge, O lovely bridge, came to

Above: Long-since gone: the old Mill Dam farm/public house, known as The Sportsman's Inn.

Barrow Gill; it runs through a band of rock. Almost at the foot of Rowling End, a well-ivied bridge. Beautiful pools and waterslides in this gill and an emminently beautiful spout and pool under the bridge. The walls of the bridge reach only to my ankles but the stonework above the arch is at least two yards. Followed this gill, winding along with Causey Pike on my left . . . Spotty Skiddaw with his chasms and ribs in sunshine looked in on me."

Twice in 1802 Coleridge walked through this favoured valley. On one occasion, it seems as though life at home had become particularly intolerable for him, as his departure was somewhat sudden. He was later to write to Sarah Hutchinson: Sunday August 1st: Half after twelve: I had a shirt, cravate, two pair of stockings, a little paper and half a dozen pens, a German Book (Voss's Poems) and a little tea and sugar, with my night-cap, packed up in my natty green oil-skin......in spite of Mrs. C. and Mary, who both raised their voices against it, especially as I left the besom scattered on the kitchen floor. Off I sailed over the bridge, through the hop-field, through the Prospect Bridge at Portinscale, and so on by the tall birch that grows out of the centre of the huge oak, along into Newlands."Then follows his description for Sarah of the beauties of this "pastoral vale", before he continues over the "antechamber"between Newlands and Buttermere.

This was followed a few weeks later by a "Glorious walk"with Tom and Mary Hutchinson: "the rain sailing along those black crags and green steeps, white as the wooly down on the under side of a willow leaf, and soft as floss silk. Silver fillets of water down every mountain from top to bottom that were as fine as a bridegroom". They scrambled up alongside Moss Force at the head of the hause, where Coleridge wrote pages of lyrical description. What, we wonder, would the farmers of Keskadale make of this poet who raptured over their "darling sheep....with their red ochre letters on their sides . . . .Bless their dear hearts, what darlings mountain sheep are!"

A few years later, the Vale of Newlands became home to Thomas Southey, brother of Robert and former Commander in the Royal Navy. By 1820 he and his wife Sarah had set up home in Emerald Bank, built on the site of an old tenement known as "Dale". There they stayed for several years, and the registers show that they brought all three of their children, Nelson Castle, Sophie Jane and Thomas Castle, to be baptised in the Chapel. Still today, almost two hundred years later, the initials SJS, delicately cut into the old glass of the bedroom window, give us the date of their daughter's birth in 1822. Thomas, in spite of his lofty social and literary associations, was not averse to being counted among the valley folk, and his name appears on the

1822 Baptismal Record for Sophie Jane Southey, daughter of Robert Southey's brother Thomas, Commander in the Royal Navy.

1825 list of Chapel wardens, though it must be said that there is no evidence that he was ever called upon to fulfill the annual position. If we are to believe Canon Hardwick Drummond Rawnsley, writing in 1901, Robert Southey loved to visit his brother, to bathe in the beck below the house, "disporting himself like any river god". A local yeoman acquaintance of Rawnsley's is credited with the observation: "He was just a girt watter dog, was Mr. Soothey,....he was terble fond of bathing thereaway, belaw t'Emerald bank". Together the brothers and their friends could talk of Bonaparte and Nelson, and world events so far away from their idyllic retreat. (Other accounts paint a less amicable relationship between the two brothers!) What is certain, however, is that among the regular summer visitors to Emerald Bank was Dr. Jowett, Master of Balliol. With groups of undergraduates known as "the Cathedrals", he would perambulate the little terrace above the meadows, which became known as "Jowett's Walk".

So, as the farmers and labourers ploughed the fields, harvested their grain and clipped their sheep, they might have glimpsed these learned gentlemen, the intellectual cream of society, walking the paths along the banks of Newlands Beck. Perhaps they might recognise another rather strange-looking gentleman whose name had spread throughout the land. William Wordsworth was a frequent visitor to the Southey household. With his sister Dorothy and his daughter Mary he wandered over the fells for many years, and one such occasion prompted him to pen the lines quoted in chapter 1, as they looked down from Catbells or Maiden Moor on to the little whitewashed chapel.

By the 1830s, countless others were admiring the fells from the dubious "comfort"of horse-driven coaches. Many ventured North, and the ride to Buttermere via Honister and over Newlands Hause became a "must-do"experience. Perhaps they were allowed a stop at "The Dog and Gun"to quench their thirst on the long journey back to Keswick. This old Public House stood at Mill Dam, where Rigg Beck now tumbles down past the site of the ancient corn mill. Back in 1804, the Newlands schoolmaster, John Marshall, had recorded in his diaries that this small establishment was kept by "an industrious widow", Mrs. Barbara Rigg. He taught her two sons Henry and John, both "exceedingly docile and well-disposed pupils". But tragedy struck twice in Barbara Rigg's life: having lost her husband Gerard in the year of their daughter Isabella's birth, she received the appalling news that her boys had been drowned in Derwentwater in 1807. Whether through illness or misadventure, her own life ended three years later .

By 1816, we find that a certain John Nicholson had taken over the provision of liquor for the new-age travellers at the "Mill Dam Inn". The Chapel Registers tell us of a baptism of Elizabeth, daughter of John Nicholson, "Innkeeper at Mill Dam"on 27th. Oct.1816. The farm at Mill Dam still existed, as we know that Joshua and Dinah Dover were raising a family there in the 1830s. The original buildings at Mill Dam, with the old valley cock-pit in the hollow below, are long since gone. The wooden-boarded house that stands there now, called just Rigg Beck, is of a much later date, as we shall see. Below it, hidden away in the trees by the water, are some of the old stones of the mill and other buildings. It is easy to see, however, that this junction of the track from Littletown and the main route towards Buttermere would have been an ideal place for a refreshment stop. By 1822 a Matthias Mumberson resided there. He is listed as Chapel warden representing Mill Dam Tenement. No mention is made of his trade, but it is surely significant to find Matthias named later in the 1929 publication of Parson and White's Directory as the victualer of "The Royal Oak"in Braithwaite. Over the page in Parson and White is the Newlands list, where Wilson Tyson is "victualer"of "The Dog and Gun."The Tysons, although numerous in surrounding areas for generations, seem to have moved into Newlands only around 1824, when Wilson Tyson also appears on the Chapel wardens rota. At that stage, he was a "slater", living at Mill Dam in a property owned by a William Edgar. Five years later he was running The Dog and Gun.

A twelve year gap in the information about the Inn and its residents brings us to the 1840s, when an up-market proprietor has changed the name to "The Sportsman", (as shown on a later map of the area in 1862.) In 1841 a son was born to Martha and Robert McGlasson, "Publican at Mill Dam". The same year saw the first really comprehensive Census of occupants of all properties throughout the country, a vital source of information to be repeated at ten-year intervals up to the present day. From this we find a whole tribe of McGlassons at High Snab. (We will meet them later.) But of Robert and Martha of Mill Dam there is no mention. In their place is Henry Lowdon, aged 30, Inn-keeper. Joshua Dover has by now moved on with his family to the farm at Littletown, and from this time on, there seems to be no further evidence of farming activities at Mill Dam.

The Lowdons settled in and prospered. Henry and his younger wife Jane found time to raise a family of 7 children, as well as attending to their inn-keeping duties. In the next census, however, taken in 1851, Henry is listed as "miner". Jane must have seen to most of the hospitality, as we learn that

Henry was in fact a manager at Goldscope, but somewhat unreliable, unable to read or write and often turning up for work drunk! Work at the mine progressed well, however, until the fatal day in Februaury 1857 when Henry Lowden was killed in a blasting accident. Ian Tyler tells us that the funeral in Keswick was attended by some 300 people, and a subscription was taken for the family's future. His wife Jane was evidently a popular character as well, for the 1861 census shows that not only was she still "Innkeeper", but had also produced an illegitimate child in 1860! Still holding the fort in 1971, she eventually disappears from view by 1874, when the Inn was run by George Graham and his wife Elizabeth.

Back in the 1840s, another name was associated with The Sportsman Inn. The "Cumberland Paquet"was the local newspaper of the time. In it, the townspeople of Keswick could occasionally read of events very close to home. There were accounts of social gatherings held by the Gentry, charitable acts carried out by wealthy ladies, and of course the ubiquitous weather reports. (Where would Cumbrians be without them?) In the January editions of 1843, we learn of the sad drowning of a young apprentice at the Pencil Works, and of the "Old Folks Saturday"with much dancing in various hostelries. On January 10th a certain Mr. John Pearson of "The Sportsman Inn nr. Keswick", was carting fagots from Brundholme Woods, when he "fell in with several bunches of primroses in full bloom". (On the same date, a blackbird's nest was found near Braithwaite with an egg already in it.) It is quite likely that Mr. Pearson was working at The Sportsman, whilst the Lowdens managed it, as a week later we hear of him again. "Jan. 17th: Several dancing parties, or what are more familiarly known as "merry nights"took place in the Neighbourhood of Keswick last week". Amongst these was one at the Low Door Inn , organised by Mr. Mossop, which was "remarkably well attended", and another by Mr. Pearson of The Sportsman Inn, "which was also a bumper.......dancing at all the Inns was kept up to a late hour and the parties were all highly delighted with the entertainment provided for them". How intriguing it is to wonder which of the Yeomen farmers and their families were included among the revellers.

However, just one month later, all their energies and resources were to be sorely taxed by a very severe winter. As reported in the Cumberland Paquet, February 21st, the people of Keswick had, "for several days past experienced a most intense frost in this part of the country, so keen indeed that not only the lakes but the rivers are covered with ice of such strength to afford ample security to the skaiters upon its glassy surface. Yesterday's indication of thaw comes very opportunely, since from the frozen state of the rivers, all the water powered machinery in this locality was threatened with an arrest".

This reference to machinery takes on a far greater significance when we look at a major change in valley life, as highlighted by the 1841 census. At Birkrigg, for example, beside the names of John Dover and his wife Jane, carrying on the farming traditions, we read of William and James Postlethwaite, lead miners, with their families. At East House, near Skelgill, Daniel Fisher was no longer a farm labourer but a lead miner, and in other places there were quarrymen and slaters. And as we have already seen, even the local hostelry was run by a miner. The huge pits and shafts which had brought such change to Newlands way back in Elizabethan times, had been recently opened up, explored and extended.

According to the authors of the "Antiquities"of 1777, Nicolson and Burn, after the departure of the German miners at the end of the 16th century there had been sporadic bursts of activity in the mines, but very little production. "These mines, it is said, served not only England but divers places beyond the sea; until the smelting houses and works were destroyed, and most of the miners slain, in the civil wars: and the works have never since been managed to any account". The legend of Cromwell's forces intervening in this way has been carried on by several writers since then, including John Postlethwaite, in "Mines and Mining in the Lake District". Records show, however, that at least some of the old mines were explored not long after the civil wars. A mining manager from Somerset, David Davies, came to work several of them, applying in 1689 for a lease from the landowner, Charles Duke of Somerset, inheritor of the Duke of Northumberland's Estates. In a letter he referred to "First, ye sand vein on Goldscope, lately discovered, where there is ore 4"thick but sore watered. Second Littledale Brow on ye same mountain where we have sunk 12 fathoms and have ore constantly....twelve men employed...ore at 50s. a ton. Third, Tinkers Hole on same moumtain..."

Further evidence points to the involvement of Thomas Robinson, Rector of Ousby, who attempted a revival of workings at Goldscope for about five years from 1697. In 1709, he published a "Natural History of Westmorland and Cumberland", in which he described the old Germanic shafts and veins, as quoted in chapter 3. He states that the Duke of Somerset has re-opened these rich veins. "Likewise smelt-houses, furnaces and all other conveniences are made ready by His Grace for setting forward a great work. But it may be presumed that the discouragement His Grace met with, which at present hath put a stop to so noble a project, was his meeting with an ignorant operator, who, not understanding the nature of the ore, burnt and destroyed fifty tun of the best Gold-Scalp ore without the production of one pound of fine copper". (Quoted by John Postlethwaite).

Very little mining seems to have been attempted during most of the eighteenth century. Parish registers in 1788 noting the burials of Edward Barren of Braithwaite and Joseph Gill of Portinscale, both killed in the mines, indicate some small-scale activities, but only after the turn of the century do we find more evidence of important developments. The technical history of the Newlands Mining ventures has been well examined by Postlethwaite, John Adams and more recently, Ian Tyler. Looking through and beyond their statistics and surveys, we can follow a change creeping over the valley, as new arrivals set up home near the mines they were working. Some of the farm buildings became homes for the miners and their families. In 1825 a John Postlethwaite was tenant in one of the Fisher's properties, whilst others of his family were listed in the farm on "Cowpers"land. The 1841 census shows William and James Postlethwaite, both leadminers, at Birkrigg with their wives and children, and a John Greener, also a miner. Alongside these newcomers, some of the younger sons of farming families also turned their hand to mining, probably from necessity at a time of great poverty and hardship amongst the labouring poor. Parish records show Joseph Fisher of Littletown and John Fisher of Akin as miners in the 1850s. Sometimes an honest and hard-working young man could "rise through the ranks". In the 1841 census, Joshua Hardisty, aged 20, was a farm labourer living in at Gill Brow with the Dover family. Two years later, Christmas Day saw the birth of little Mary Hardisty to Joshua and his wife Sarah nee Dover, all living at Birkrigg, with Joshua now a quarryman. Still at Birkrigg in the 1861 census, he was head of his household, a miner, and was surrounded by Dovers ranging from his 88 yr. old mother-in-law, Sarah's 67yr. old uncle, to an assortment of aunts, cousins and nephews. In many rural areas, miners and quarrymen were the roughest and lowest members of the community, despised by their farming neighbours and renowned for drunkeness and violence. This could hardly have been true of those who settled in Newlands. We even read of a couple of miners who worked so high up towards Dale Head fell that they built themselves a hut and slept there five nights a week. Like many others, they were keen "carders", and from a local family legend comes the story that a group of dalesmen trekked up there now and then for a rubber, taking with them a sackful of potatoes as a present. The danger and unpleasantness of working conditions for Newlands miners were real enough, but at least there were family and friends to give support after accidents or injury.

During this period, leases for working the mines were constantly changing hands, as one after another optimistic prospector thought he could make his fortune, only to face debt and bankruptcy. Some of these men came from a distance, others were more local. A licence was granted in 1845 to John Dixon of Borrowdale to "search for, work, and get all or any of the Mines, Veins or Seams of Lead, Lead ore, Copper and Copper ore within, under or upon the Lands or Grounds called Dale Head and Gold Scope........bounded on the North West by the Rivulet called Kiskadale and extending on the South East from Newlands Chapel by Little Town End to the extremity of the Boundary where it joins Borrowdale."John Dixon agreed to yield one full twelfth part of any ore raised, to Major general Henry Wyndham, a natural son of the 3rd. Earl of Egremont, and inheritor of the Cumberland Estates. He paid one pound for the licence, which was granted for only two years. In 1847 a private company took over the lease, spent far too much money constructing costly machinery, and were forced to sell at the end of eighteen months, with a loss in the area of £5,000.

It was in 1847 that Mannex and Whelan produced yet another directory of the area. They apparently had heard a little of the contemporary explorations, and described the situation in this way: "At Huithwaite, (Yewthwaite) is a lead mine, where immense quantities of ore have been raised, but it is now very poor.....here are also two exhausted copper mines, Viz. Goldscap and Dale Head, the former of which is said to have contained a vein of gold, but it has not been wrought since the reign of Elizabeth. Dale Head mine was wrought a few years ago by the late Mr. Sheffield, mineral agent to the Duke of Devonshire, who obtained considerable quantities of rich grey, purple and green malachite ore; but after erecting a smelt mill, and incurring other heavy expenses, the work was given up. A quarry of fine roofing slate has recently been opened at the head of the vale".

Further down the valley, there was a great increase in activity at the Stoneycroft mine. The Keswick Mining Company, re-opening the ancient works of "The Old Men", the name given to their 17th century precursors, hoped to find evidence and remains of a legendary Stoneycroft catastrophe. Centuries earlier, miners had built a dam high up the beck, diverted the water, sunk a shaft and discovered rich ore. But at some stage, hidden in history, the

The legacy of the Barrow Mines: Ugly screes on the fellside with lumpy, boggy remnants of mine workings above Uzzicar.

dam burst and men were buried alive in the mud and rocks. Research done by Mr. Wildridge of Workington suggests that the only surviving reference to this flood is in a letter written in the 1690s from David Davies, the mining manager, to the Duke of Somerset. Small wonder that tales have been shrouded in mystery ever since! However, looking at parish registers, there is even room to wonder whether, years before Davies arrived, this flood was the cause of the deaths of Richard Fisher of Snabb and Matthew Bell of Skelgill. Their burials took place on 18th March, 1626, when it was recorded that they were both "kild in the mynes."Is it a coincidence that a few days later, Danyell Hechstetter "the yonger"and Samuell Hechstetter, sons of the original German miners, were also buried in Crosthwaite? In 1846 The Keswick Mining Company found some ancient tools and lengths of thick chain, but none of the hoped-for human remains. (Think what we might have learned with modern DNA science!) They sunk the shaft deeper, put in a 22ft. water-wheel, and improved a two-mile track leading up above the beck to Sail and Scar Crags. A tramway was constructed to carry wagons, a smelt-mill and a crushing plant installed, but the Stoneycroft workings never really fulfilled their ancient promise of riches!

Other hillsides around the valley were also yielding moderate amounts of ore by the 1850s. At Yewthwaite, high above Littletown, work was carried on for a few years by a dozen or so miners for Messrs. Clarke, Chapman & Co, with some success, but when a valuable deposit was discovered at Goldscope in 1853, Yewthwaite's workforce dwindled to four, and the mine was closed again. The next stage there, in the 1860s, invoved the sinking of a new level, and the installation of a Steam Engine to raise water and ore. By 1876, however, yet another set of new owners faced bankruptcy. 1883 saw the establishment of the Yewthwaite and Newlands United Mine Company, under the supervision of Henry Vercoe, a mining engineer from Portinscale, but even then mis-management and neglect dogged the efforts of this and subsequent private companies.

A similar tale can be told concerning the years following the "Great Brunch"at Goldscope, in the boom years of 1853/4: a few years of profit, but ultimately too much danger and expense. The mine was eventually abandoned in 1864. On the hillsides of Barrow, above Uzikar Farm, we cannot fail nowadays to notice the ugly screes, landslips and boggy foot-lands that are the legacy of mining there. The "Sandy vein", as it was called, contained so much unstable, slippery quartz particles, that even the efforts of Henry Vercoe, with first a 20-horse power and then a 75 horse-power engine, a 60ft. water- wheel and shafts of 80 fathoms, did not sustain the profitable production longer than five and a half years. At about this time, we learn of local discontent and opposition to some of these mining developments. In 1869 The Derwent Angling association took the Goldscope Mining Company to court with a charge of pollution of the waters. (150 years on, the question of the pollution of Derwentwater and Bassenthwaite stills rides high in local projects.)

Finally, a comment from John Postlethwaite in his 1913 account of Lake District mining. He is writing of the Dale Head Mine, high up into the hills beyond the farms, where recently a Mr. Barron of Keswick had prospected: "Mr. Barron was very successful while the mine was in his hands; indeed it is said that if he had sold the ore in its raw state he would have realised a small fortune; but he tried to grasp a larger profit by smelting the ore and selling it in a manufactured state, and, like the Duke of Somerset, met with an ignorant operator by whose unskilful manipulation the ore was partly destroyed, or reduced to a condition from which he and his workmen were unable with their unskilful and unscientific methods to produce marketable copper".

With this brief summary of mining activities in Newlands, we have reached the turn of the century. But only a small percentage of the valley population was ever involved directly in the mine workings. As it became more and more difficult in the mid-eighteen hundreds for farmers to support their large families, or for younger sons to inherit enough land to make farming profitable, so the census returns reflect a marked difference in a way of life that had remained virtually unchanged for four centuries. At High Snab in 1841, the McGlasson family had moved in, but only Samuel, aged 30, was farming. Thomas and John McGlasson were wood-managers, while brother James was a tea-dealer! Their residency, however, was short-lived, as ten years later the farm buildings were shared by John Clark and John Bowness, both farmers.

The close-knit community at Littletown perhaps witnessed the most dramatic changes in occupancy, but at the same time held on to its farming legacies. Those two ancient families, the Dovers and the Wrens, had lived there for some time by 1841. Joshua Dover and his wife Dinah continued the work of old Henry and Sarah. Peter Wren, listed in the census as "Independent", was head of the Wren household, with son Joseph, wife and family. (We will look more closely at Peter's life in the next chapter.) One of the several John Fishers was living there as a labourer, while most of the Fisher clan were up at Skelgill. In 1851, the Dovers had moved on, and Joseph and Elizabeth Wren had new neighbours in the shape of Wilson Tyson, quarryman, and William Hodgson, miner. (Tyson, being only 32 years of age at this point, cannot have been the same character who had turned up at The Dog and Gun in 1829! Presumably his son.) Ten years later, and alongside the farmers, miners and quarrymen, we find Isaac Jackson, schoolmaster, lodged at Littletown with his wife Jane and family.

But by far the most intriguing newcomer was the new incumbent, the Rev. George Tandy, aged 41, born in Calcutta, India! Without knowing his background, it is impossible here to guess at how long he had lived in England or how, in 1861, he came to be Curate of such a remote chapel. His wit and talents were demonstrated in contributions of both sketch and verse to "Punch", and his spirited talk and humour must have brought new life into vestry meetings, where he took over the "Chair" to discuss such matters as a new burial ground around the church, with the old-timers Fisher Thwaite, John Dover and Joseph Wren. Apparently, he lost his private fortune in the "Overend and Gurney" bank smash, and sadly for the valley had to seek a richer living. In Newlands his stipend was just £70 a year, but on top of that he had shared his own wealth generously with his parishioners.

The changes in the fortunes of Newlands families and the shifting pattern of occupations over these mid-nineteenth century years, reflects the struggle that farmers were having all over the area. In Newlands, some at least had the opportunity to adapt to other work. But generally in the North-West this was a time of great rural poverty and hardship. Others have described the situation graphically. Hugh Walpole brings into "Rogue Herries"some depressing details of life for the average farm labourer: "The agricultural labourer at this time earned fourteen pence a day or eight shillings a week, and his wife, if she were lucky, might earn sixpence a day. Here are some of the things a labourer must provide for his family: candles, 3d; bread or flour 1s. 8d; yeast and salt 4d; soap, starch 2 1/2d; tea, sugar, butter, 1s; thread, worsted, 3d. The weekly total would be some 8s. 4 1/2d, or £21. 15. 6. per annum, his earnings being £20. 16s. In addition to the weekly expenses there were clothing, rent, fuel, amounting to some £8, and leaving the happy villager with a yearly deficiency of nearly £9. He could not brew small beer save for some special occasion. So difficult was it to obtain soap for washing that they burned green fern and kneaded it into balls."Admittedly, most of the farm labourers in Newlands were related in some way to the farmers themselves, and were therefore better provided for. Walpole also wrote, of his character David Herries, "David found that here in all the country that stretched between Uldale and Carlisle matters were very different from the independence and security of the Statesmen in Borrowdale and Newlands. There, a labourer could rise by thrift and diligence until he should be in some sort his own master."Although Walpole's work is fiction, the depiction of the misery in rural areas is based on fact. In 1834 the Poor Law Amendment Act was passed. In many areas destitute families were split, sent to hop fields, to factories or if all else failed, to the workhouses. In Cumberland and Westmorland there was at least opportunity for servant work on farms, washing clothes, and seasonal labour. There were few salaried overseers of the poor, and many local farmers would help with employment. The Poor Rate was established, with tenants and owners alike obliged to contribute. Beggars, starving children, lame ex-soldiers and tramps roamed the countryside. Contemporary accounts describe Irish Labourers coming over for the reaping season, "potters", or travellers, hawking their wares from town to town, and abandoned mothers with illegitimate children being moved from one parish to another. No parish wanted to pay for the poor of other areas. Dorothy Wordsworth wrote compassionately in her journals of wives separated from husbands by war, and of tall, amazonian women of the potters' trade with "little bare-footed children"wandering the countryside.

In the market towns, vagrants and pickpockets were abusive and threatening. J.W.Pringle's report of 1834 to the Commissioners of the Poor Laws in Cumberland and Westmorland mentioned that "such persons are frequently very troublesome at detached farms and cottages, in a manner demanding money, conduct which constables in the rural districts are quite inefficient to prevent". This "Terror of the Tramp"meant that sometimes genuine labourers seeking work were in danger of being thrown into the Vagrancy wards, as the danger of the spread of cattle disease was just as frightening. In the one year 1848, in an area stretching from Keswick to the region north of Bassenthwaite Lake, a report to the General Board of Health in Keswick recorded an incredible figure of 42,000 vagrants! This was probably an exceptionally high number in a time of widespread depression, but gives an idea of the miserable state of the poor. The Poor Law Union of Cockermouth was responsible for the overseeing of the needy in the Keswick region, but help came from other sources too

The "Cumberland Paquet"of the 1840s regularly featured the progress of charitable causes and funds set up for the relief of the poor of Keswick. One, the "Pipers' Soup Fund", ran for years. Other organisations offered cartloads of coal, sides of beef, or bundles of clothing. In sharp contrast to the prevailing poverty, those whose circumstances were favourable led an increasingly lively social life. We read of the "Independent Order of Oddfellows belonging to Keswick,"who held a Ball at the "new and commodious Lodge Room in that town", when surplus proceeds were added to the Fund for Widows and Orphans belonging to the Lodge". There was tea and refreshments, and "dancing was kept up with great Spirit".

In Newlands too, there were some startling contrasts of wealth and poverty. Undoubtedly, some would fit in with the keen observations of Miss Harriet Martineau, reformer, philosopher, writer and tireless campaigner, living in Ambleside in 1844: "The decline in the fortunes of the statesmen (estatesmen) as they are locally called, has been regular and mournful to witness". She describes the demise of old families: "Since the Union of Scotland with England, and the consequent extinction of border warfare, these Dalesmen have become the quietest people in the world. No more summoned to war, nothing calls them out of their retreats, except an occasional market, or a sale of household furniture in some neighbouring valley. They go on practising their old-fashioned methods of tillage and herding, living in their primitive abodes, and keeping up customs, and even a manner of speech, which are elsewhere almost obsolete. It will not be so for long. Their agriculture cannot hold its ground against modern improvements. Their homespun linen and cloth do not answer now in comparison with Manchester cottons and Yorkshire woollens. Their sons part off to the manufacturing districts, to get a better maintenance than they can find at home, and the daughters must go out to service. Still the old croft will not support those who remain; the land is mortgaged more deeply. The interest cannot be raised; and under this pressure the temptation to the sinking Dalesman to drown his cares in drink, becomes too strong for many a one who has no resources of education to fall back upon. Then comes the end - the land and furniture are sold, the family disperse, and a stranger comes in."

Certainly, some families did disappear from Newlands around this time, but as we shall see, the second half of the nineteenth century brought success for others.

Chapter 11
Old Statesmen, New School

The fortunes of Mr. Joseph Fisher of Portinscale, whom we met when, in 1856, he benevolently presented £100 to be used for the benefit of Newlands Chapel Sunday School, were far removed from those of Harriet Martineau's local farmers. Just two years later, in 1858, Joseph was busy again. Isaac Jackson the schoolmaster copied out yet another deed. This time, Mr. Fisher had agreed with the Charity Commissioners that the sum of £150 could be invested, with the following provisos: that ten shillings would go to the Incumbent of Newlands and his successors for preaching a sermon annually in the Chapelry of Newlands on the Thursday following Whitsuntide, "and the residue of such dividends and income at their and his discretion, to and among the deserving poor and needy inhabitants of Newlands". Subsequently, on 1st July, the perpetual Curate, John

Above: Birkrigg Cottage, home of Peter and Betty Wren in 1850, scene of many a social gathering.

Monkhouse, his two Chapelwardens Reuben Grave and John Gaskarth, and a collection of 15 other reliable gentlemen, sent a letter of thanks for his kindness and liberality, assuring him that all who partook of his munificence in the future would fully appreciate it and retain a grateful remembrance of his benefits!

Joseph Fisher was born in Newlands in 1782. As we know, the Fishers were of ancient lineage, and farmed in several locations. Some prospered more than others, so we read of Yeomen, Independent Gentlemen, husbandmen, labourers and miners amongst their nineteenth century descendants. They were here to stay for a long while yet. Other families, too, managed to carry on in the valley in spite of the crumbling farming economy. Littletown was home to several generations of the Wren family, with Peter and his wife Ann, a Clark from Buttermere, raising a lively clutch of youngsters there at the beginning of the century. As time went on, their four sons followed careers that well demonstrated the contrasting opportunities of the times. Eldest son Joseph carried on the farming at Littletown; second son Abraham moved into Keswick to work at the Pencil Factory; third son John, reportedly after a family disagreement, went off to join the Life Guards in London; and young Peter used his brains and confidence to work firstly in a drapery in London, but then to profit from the Plantations out in the West Indies.

A wealth of fascinating information about his subsequent return to Newlands, marriage to Betty Mawson of Emerald, and life of leisure, sport and entertaining, is found in a little gem of a book, "Uncle Peter", by Abraham Wren Rumney. Only a few closely guarded copies of this, a lovingly written testimony by a great-nephew, are hidden away in cupboards and archives! From it emerges a vivid picture of this legendary dalesman and his acquaintances.

Peter, over forty years old but still unmarried after his world travels, was enjoying a "short"holiday in Newlands, when he met Betty Mawson, sister of old Moses and some years his senior. The story has it that she took matters into her own hands with the question, "Dusta think thoo need ga back, Peter?"The outcome of which was that the pair married and settled into the old house at Birkrigg. Now almost derelict, probably soon to become a holiday cottage, it was a small but fine home in 1850, with its elegant front door, "drawing room"and two bedrooms on the high level, and steep stairs down to the house-place and kitchen. On the stony ground outside, Peter grew lettuce, mint herbs and a few potatoes, while a hen-house and some beehives completed the picture. Both Peter and Betty had money to invest, so with no need to earn a living, the newest resident of Birkrigg spent his time socialising, fishing, tramping the lanes and entertaining his neighbours.

The writer of the book tells of supper parties for up to thirty card-players, (whist and "lant"being taken very seriously in the valley), when statesmen, farm-hands and miners alike would share in the fun. "The first meal, tea, was taken about four o'clock, and was usually only attended by the elders and non-farmers, as the "younger end"had their milking and other jobs to attend to. "Best caps"were the wear for the elder ladies, and on one occasion Betty was terribly put about by finding that the cat had displaced the band-box lid and produced five kittens in the precious headgear".

We also learn of Peter's chapel attendances: "He was a great churchman, and as a boy I used to think he actually competed with the priest in both loudness and pace. Certainly he used to get far ahead in the Lord's Prayer and the Creed, while in alternating the Psalms he was finishing the second sentence as the rest of the congregation was entering it". Occasionally, however, Peter would steal out of the chapel mid-way through and be seen tearing down the lonning (lane): "Peter's bees ha' kessen"would be the whisper round the chapel, as he rushed away to attend to his swarming hive. Fortunately, the priest, the Rev. George Tandy was a good friend and walking companion of Peter's.

Peter's brother Joseph, staying at Littletown, was the only one of the four Wren lads to continue the family tradition of sheep farming. Years later, an old friend of Peter's, Samuel Ladyman, would remember Joseph in his "Thoughts and Recollections of Keswick": "Joseph Wren of Newlands died in the same house in which he was born, over 80yrs. of age. These three, (a Miss Younghusband and a Miss Elleray,) were never from home over two months in all their lifetime". The 1871 census shows Joseph with his sons and grandsons still at Littletown.

Further up the valley, another of Peter's elderly neighbours also claimed higher status than the average farmer. "The old lord"lived in a very ancient, damp, small farm building annexed to Akin, which by then belonged to Peter's brother Abraham. The title, held in those days by yet another John Fisher, was on paper only, as "t'auld lword"was in fact one of the poorest tenants. His pedigree, however, stretched way back into the old Fisher family. "Lord's tenement"is one of the ancient names in the Chapel Wardens' rota, and very often over the years a Fisher lived there. The title came with the ownership of a few acres in the valley where the lord was historically entitled, by "ancient freehold", to any minerals found in the land. Throughout the rest of Newlands, they were the property of the lord of the manor. At Akin, John had created a vegetable garden producing "taties"and berries, while his wife made moss-besoms to sell in the dale and at Keswick market at the price of threepence each, or sixpence for a superior one. John's contribution to chapel worship, in his younger days, had been to play a bassoon up in the gallery, with violins accompanying, but in Rumney's recollections, by the mid- 1800s music was provided by a harmonium. According to Rumney, John Fisher was "a man of great stature, and on one of his not infrequent sprees amused himself by changing a quantity of the signs of the inns and shops in Keswick. His foot was reputed to be sixteen inches long; and if repute exaggerated, his clogs were so notable that he considered it a sufficient payment for his doctor's services to promise them to him on his death"!

Wealth of a far more material nature was evident in the Mawson family of Emerald, home of Peter Wren's wife Elizabeth. The first Moses Mawson in Newlands came, as we learn from his will, from a prosperous family in Bromfield in the late seventeen hundreds. He married Jane Robinson, and came to live at Low Snab, then still often referred to as Little Dale. He and Jane produced nine children, all but one of whom survived well into the mid-eighteen hundreds. As we saw earlier, Thomas Southey and his family lived at Emerald in the 1820s, but by 1830 Moses Mawson, junior, had moved in there with his new wife Sarah. At Emerald bank he surpassed the achievements of his father by raising a family of eleven! By 1850 Newlands was teeming with Aunts, Uncles and Cousins, including Moses senior and Moses junior, his brother William and family, and sister Jane who had married John Dover and so continued that family line. On the night of the 1851 census, Emerald was "home"not only to a very large family, but also to two Merchants from the City of London! Herein lies the key to the family prosperity: the Mawsons never were solely reliant on fellside farming, but always had business connections. Later records show that some of the third generation left the valley for good in the later years of the century, and sought their fortunes out in Australia and New Zealand. Today it is still possible to see at Emerald, which is privately owned, the wide, levelled area on the slope above the house where the Mawsons' carriage would rest, with the stables for their horses a little way across the field.

In contrast, John Dover, husband of Jane Mawson, had farming roots stretching way back to William Dover of 1574. His father, Henry, was a product of generations of Dover/Fisher/Thwaite/Mayson/Towlson marriages, and had introduced a new combination of families by marrying Sarah Grave from Skelgill. It would seem that Henry moved around frequently, as the parish registers name various farms as the birth-places of his nine children, including Low House, Littletown, Gillbrow and even The Vicarage. His eldest son John, after his marriage to Jane Mawson, also worked at several farms, with their sons Henry and Moses born at Low Snab and Skelgill. Eventually the family settled for many years at Birkrigg. His brothers Reuben and Joshua also continued farming in Newlands, but had to supplement their incomes by taking on other jobs. Another of the Dover lads, Joseph, seized the chance through a distant family connection to travel over the hills to Temple Sowerby, where he became the village Tanner, and married into the vicar's family. The Dovers in Newlands had always taken on responsibilities as Chapel wardens, and John continued this tradition, along with Reuben and Joshua. It was during one of John's duties as Chapelwarden that another very important step was taken in the valley.

During the curacy of the Rev. John Monkhouse, and with considerable financial support from him, a schoolhouse was erected at the West end of the chapel. The wardens' accounts give a list of subscribers, including influential people like General Wyndham of Cockermouth, (who features on many a contemporary petition as the Duke of Northumberland's Agent), the Speddings of Mirehouse and a Sir John Woodford. The total raised from subscriptions was £37.0.6. The practical hard work, however, was carried out by the locals; the memorandum of 1841 stating, "all the materials were conveyed to the place by the inhabitants of Newlands at their own expense."

This must have meant a significant improvement in the education of the dozens of Newlands children. They had for many generations received a very basic education in words and numbers from either the Chapel incumbent, (often the only clerk in the whole area), or from one of the itinerant schoolmasters serving several dales. Parish records tell of a Mr. Brisco in the Keswick in 1678, of John Atkinson the curate, who witnessed many farmers' wills in the early 18th century, and of Joseph Fisher of Littletown whom we have already met. One well-educated holder of the position, a John Walker who later went on to teach at Loweswater, wrote a poem "The Village Pedagogue". In 1804, John Marshall was teaching the younger Dovers, Thwaites and Fishers in the chapel vestry or out in the open air. He was paid £10 a year and given free board and lodging at a nearby farm. This arrangement seemed to suit Mr. Marshall very well. He wrote, "I was as much elated as if I had been appointed a Teller of the Exchequer.....I lived in peace with all mankind. My vacant hours were dedicated to reading, music, tracing rivulets to their source and ascending mountains. Content soothed my pillow, and uninterrupted friendship with all my neighbours sweetened each revolving day". The late George Bott has described this idyllic existence, adding that John Marshall contrived to bring some awareness of the outside world into the valley: at the expense of Lord William Gordon, living at Derwent Bay, John had London newspapers delivered to local farmers, who passed them round the valley in rotation before passing them back to him. After John Marshall came others including Jonathan Dixon, who lived at Mill Dam and whose daughter Sophie Jane was baptised in 1822.

The next generation of children was treated, in 1837, to new school tables. An entry in the chapel wardens' accounts shows that Robert Dixon, the joiner and carpenter at Swinside, was paid £1.2.2. for making them. At this stage we get a clue as to how the parish financed practical necessities: the accounts of the following year state that "it was also agreed that a rate of 2d in the pound be collected to defray the expenses incurred in repairing the School Tables, Chapel Windows and the wall of the Chapel Yard, in addition to the usual 4 per cent."

To squeeze the new tables into the tiny vestry, or even at the back of the chapel must have caused problems, as it was just four years later that we read of the building of the new schoolroom. By 1847, an entry in the Mannex and Whelan "Gazetteer"of Cumberland noted, "attached to the church is a neat school, built chiefly by subscription; and the incumbent guarantees £40 a year to the master". With the new school came a new master, John Simpson, aged 25 and lodging at Emerald Bank with Moses and Sarah Mawson and their seven children. Perhaps it was in appreciation of his services that their eighth child, born two years later, was baptised Simpson Wren Mawson. John may have been related to a large family of Simpsons living across the valley at Swinside at that time. There, the census records another John, aged 40, with his wife Mary and no fewer than ten children from the age of fifteen down to six months! Our valiant master had enough pupils from just the Mawsons and the Simpsons to fill his little schoolroom! Then follows a mystery: by 1851 the Simpsons have all vanished! The only reminder of the whole family in the census records is the presence of young Simpson Mawson, now with younger brothers and sisters. (The year 1885 will provide us with a clue as to what might have happened!)

In the schoolmaster's shoes is Isaac Jackson, with his wife Jane and family at Littletown. The 1861 census tells us that he was born in Drigg, and his wife in Northumberland. Isaac copied out the deeds recording Mr. Joseph Fisher's gift to the Sunday school and to the Poor of Newlands in the 1850s, and wrote the letters of thanks. In 1862 a detailed map of the valley clearly marked the school as part of the chapel building. By 1866, however, the Jacksons had moved on. Perhaps the youngsters from the Newlands farms were too much of a challenge, as Tom Spark, schoolmaster in 1866 was swiftly followed in 1868 by Mr. William Castley. The Rev. R. Rutherford along with his two wardens Messrs. Thwaite and Wren, unanimously decided that Mr. Castley should be appointed to the office of vestry Clerk, "for the purpose of entering minutes and otherwise assisting at the meetings, without salary".

Sadly, we have no records of how Mr. Castley went about his teaching. He chaired the Vestry meetings, held in the schoolroom, until 1871, when he retired to take up some other (perhaps better paid?) work. The Rev. Rutherford then moved that "the thanks of the meeting be accorded to Mr.Castley, the retiring master, expressing their regret at his leaving, and thanking him for his attention and ability in discharging the duties of his office, and expressing a hope that he may be long spared to exercise his usefulness in his new sphere of labour".

This same meeting had been called expressly for the purpose of appointing managers for the school. Four were to be instated forthwith, then two would retire by rotation each year when others would be elected. So it came about that, three hundred years after Thwaites, Dovers, Hodgsons and Fishers were "hedge-lookers"and "constables"in Rogersett, their direct descendants became "school-lookers"! With the appointment of school managers came the application for an annual allowance under the new education acts. One of the requirements by law for the running of the school was that a log- book should be kept by the head teacher. It is thanks to this that we discover more than ever about daily life in the heart of Newlands.

"The diary or log-book must be stoutly bound and contain not less than 300 ruled pages.

The principal teacher must make at least once a week in the log-book an entry which will specify ordinary progress, visits of managers, and other facts ...such as the dates of withdrawals, commencements of duty, cautions, illness &c.,

No reflections or opinions of a general nature are to be entered into the log-book."

Inside the front are details of the employment of one of the teachers,

The tiny schoolroom under the mountains.

Mrs. Foster. She had taught at Alston, Crosthwaite and Blencairn before coming to Newlands, where she remained from 1881 until 1904.

The teacher who opened the school on January 15th 1877 was Miss. J. Barwine. Her first entry reads: "Opened the school this morning and admitted nine." The school managers, Mr. Wilson and Mr. Dover, looked in. Her initial impression of her pupils was not very complimentary: "Children: Found they were not accustomed to Standard work. The infants knew nothing".

However, things began to improve in the second week, with the comment that "the children know their own classes"! The following week, Miss Barwine was to encounter one of the major hazards of her career in Newlands: "Tuesday: The schoolroom nearly covered with water when I came in, owing to the downfall of rain which had been during the night". (Over 30 years later, in January 1908, the yearly report was again to begin with the news that the schoolroom was half flooded and the cloakroom completely flooded).

Gradually things got sorted out, a blackboard was provided, the girls' sewing improved, and those children who could make it to school through the snow and floods began to show promise. More pupils arrived from time to time. On one occasion little John Thwaite arrived with his sister, who informed Miss Barwine that John was taking the place of his brother, who was no longer coming! Arithmetical cards, which had been on order for a month, eventually arrived, the children were introduced to "drill", ("which pleases them very much") and the new school mistress seemed quite pleased.

At the beginning of April we read, "Some of the children from school, it being Easter Monday". No two weeks' holiday in those days! Examinations loomed large in the scholars' lives, with inspectors arriving regularly at the school to study progress. Miss Barwine struggled to introduce "letters"to a stream of infants who had never encountered them. Not all children appreciated her efforts: "All working very fairly except Elizabeth Wilkinson who will not do anything for me". The first annual Inspector's Report was very encouraging. Copied carefully into the log-book by John Wilson, it tells us that "The instruction and discipline are really credible and speak well for the Mistress' intelligence and zeal. The reading is intelligent and fluent, the handwriting and spelling good and the arithmetic accurate. Next year I hope that Grammar and Geography will be taken up. The singing must be improved."

In August that year, school resumed after the summer holiday. But things were not quite according to plan. Miss Barwine wrote, "Intended coming back at the end of the month, but owing to the weather being so wet, and people could not get their hay, the Management thought we had better have another week". This, of course, was because so many of the older children would be involved in the harvest, and would certainly not have shown up. Even when term did start, attendance was poor, as "all the hay is not got yet". This state of affairs dragged on for several weeks. It must have been a frustrating time for Miss Barwine. Eventually things returned to normal, the schoolroom was cleaned, "texts"were put up on the walls, and attendances improved. Truancy did, however, feature in the valley: "One of the girls has missed school all this week, and when I enquired about her, her Master told me he had sent her to school every day". There were times, too, when the farm servants had a holiday, and then the girls were kept at home to work. Other rival attractions to tempt the children away from school were the running of the hounds, bleaberry picking and the farming activities of sheep washing and clipping.

On these important occasions, it was "all hands to the sheep". Neighbours gathered at each others' farms to help, with the skilled clippers

Winter in Newlands: no wonder the children struggled to get to school!

seated on tressels, the older boys dragging the sheep over to them, and the younger ones gathering the wool. The women and girls would be fully occupied providing jugs of beer all day and a good feast at night. At the end of each day, drinking and dancing would go on well into the night. No wonder the little schoolroom was missing a few of its pupils at this time every year!

In November 1877 two new children came to the school. Records stated that they had moved in to The Mill Dam Inn. Sure enough, George Graham had taken over the running of "The Sportsman"that year, and the two newcomers would probably be Margaret and William, aged 8 and 7. The frequent arrivals and departures of different pupils would be a constant problem for Newlands teachers over the years.

Miss Barwine struggled on, tackling the cold and damp by lighting the schoolroom fire in the mornings (only to fill the place with smoke), facing complete chaos after the 1878 summer repairs, suggesting that a urinal should be provided for the boys' yard, and trying to coax responses from her "nervous"and shy infants. Her writing becomes unruly under the stress, as she records in despair "I have given them all the time I could", and, after a school inspection, "I do not think the children did as well as I expected; I did my best for them". Sadly, it all seems to have been too much for Miss Barwine, and on Friday 17th June we read, "Am going to close the school today for midsummer holiday. It will be re-opened by a new teacher".

Miss Mary Alice Mills, aged only 22, made a promising start in spite of stormy weather, a dirty schoolroom and sickly children. However, by May

1880, the inspector was not at all satisfied with the standard of reading and spelling, which had "declined considerably and are seriously defective". Mary Alice battled on. In February 1881, "the scholars are writing in their copy books for the first time since Xmas. The ink has been frozen."Four new panes of glass were put in the broken windows, the children were taught the Comparison of Adjectives, Simple Division and Scripture texts. By 1881 the inspector was impressed: "Great pains have evidently been taken to remedy the defects mentioned last year, and with generally good success". For Mary Alice, however, life in the Valley was not what she wanted. She handed in her resignation on November 4th.

With the arrival of Mrs. Jane Foster four days later, a long, settled time of teaching was established. She was to remain with the farmers' children until 1903, continuing even after a one- month break for the birth of her son Robert in 1883. The log book continues to provide a detailed picture of the hardships of life, the constant battle with illness, damp and dirt, the deteriorating conditions of the school buildings and the fluctuating standards of the education for the next twenty years. The fortunes of several families are reflected in the progress, or otherwise, of their children. Truants and miscreants are named and shamed, prize-winners are congratulated, families leave the valley and others arrive. Throughout it all Mrs. Foster lovingly tends her flock, berating their idleness or rudeness, encouraging their painful attempts to grasp reading and spelling, and, so very often, bemoaning the lack of exercise books, the rickety desks and dirty conditions.

Milestones in community life are recorded now and then. On Monday Jan. 20th 1882, the children were given a holiday to attend the funeral of Mr. John Graves, and in 1883 for that of Mr. Peter Wren, both senior and greatly respected gentlemen. Holidays were also given for the Braithwaite Sheep Fair, for "Band of Hope"excursions, and, on June 3rd 1885, for the grand opening of the newly restored Chapel. The following year the children had an unexpected visit or from America. A Mr. Simpson called in to see them. He gave each child 2d. and "seemed very pleased with their work". This would be none other than the Mr. J.B. Simpson who was recorded in 1885 as the chief contributor to the cost of the Chapel renovations. He had lived at Swinside as a boy with his nine younger brothers and sisters, before the disappearance of the whole family. It would seem that they had emigrated to America!

The school managers called in every week, with Moses Dover succeeding his father John, the younger John Wilson taking over from the senior, and Joshua Wren also taking his turn. They were, however, somewhat negligent in ensuring the comfort of the children, as year after year Mrs. Foster had to complain of leaking roofs, broken windows, dirty floors and lack of essential supplies! On top of which, she was not always inspired by her pupils' attitudes. John Blockley's behaviour was so bad that his mother was called in, and his brother Samuel "had to be brought by force to school". Mr. Blockley was a lead-miner from Worthing, living at High Snab with his six children, who had been moved around from place to place. For them, school was not a pleasant experience! William Bell would not learn his tables and "doesn't care", Mary Thwaite was chastised for sulking, and Harry Hodgson would not do his homework. When we learn that one of the stumbling blocks for Sarah Grace Thwaite was to "reduce 2 miles to inches", we can sympathise!

Another regular visitor to the school was the resident clergyman. The vicars seemed to have responsibility for teaching and testing the scholars on Religious knowledge. Their reports were usually extremely complimentary. They played their part, too, in providing some entertainment and fun for the youngsters. Every year they would hold a Christmas and a summer "tea-party". The Rev. and Mrs. Whitehead gave a "magic lantern"show before they left Newlands in 1885, and their successors the Rev. and Mrs. Armstrong regularly invited the children to the vicarage.

Occasionally some of the "superior"ladies of the valley would look in; the unmarried Misses Mawson and their friends, and the Misses Dover. One former pupil of the school, Jane Ann Dover, gave regular help with weekly visits to teach the children new songs.

And so the years went by. Every July the teacher complained that the older children were away at sheep clipping; -"so many children invited to go to the neighbours' houses". Every August and September meant absences because the hay was not yet gathered in. When the children did manage to reassemble they had invariably "forgotten all they knew". Winter after winter brought flooded rooms and blocked roads; -"snow so thick that the children had to be taken home in carts". The winter of 1886 brought the most extreme conditions. Right through until March, snowstorms blocked the roads and cut off the fell farms. The children who did try to struggle in to school, were coming from homes of hardship and misery. In the Carlisle Journal we read of treacherous conditions for the ice-skaters on Derwentwater, and of the inhabitants of Wythburn having used all available fuel and wood and left without fire for 14 days. But the report on March 9th sums up the situation back at home for our Newlands children: "The weather is causing much trouble and loss to the farmers, a great number of sheep being lost in the snow, while the demands on the haystacks is very serious. Many of the farmers are out of hay, and one of the hill farmers is paying £40 for sheep hay alone. The storms of the past week have exceeded in severity anything remembered for over 30 years."

Disasters were not always linked to winter weather. In the summer of 1888 no doubt school lessons were interrupted by the news of a fire in a hay-barn at Low Snab farm, the home of pupils Thomas and Margaret Jackson. The newspaper reported that "a mounted messenger was dispatched to Keswick, and within a short time the fire engine was manned and on its way. The damage to the building and stock, estimated at £10, was covered by insurance".

The dreaded inspectors came and went, leaving varying reports of satisfaction or discontent:- "A brisk and cheerful tone pervades the school and the instruction has evidently been careful and intelligent"(1884). "Order is good and manners pleasant"(1890). "Considering special difficulties of the year owing to severe weather, the results of the examination are on the whole creditable. Discipline is not of a very high order and the children talked unchecked......a couple of suitable desks for the infants should be provided as recommended last year."(1895). Sadly, as the century drew to a close, the little school and its teacher were struggling to keep up to standard: "Much benefit would probably be derived from the adoption of some more modern methods of instruction; discipline should improve"(1898). Conditions were still primitive, and the building still freezing: "A thermometer should be hung in the schoolroom"(1900).

1901 saw the arrival of a new, very strict school inspector. He and Mrs. Foster had a set-to when he complained that the register was being called at 10.45am. instead of 10.0am, and proceeded to cancel the morning's attendance record. Mrs. Foster wrote, "As we have no clock going for about 6 months, it seems a difficult thing to know the exact time for marking the registers. The school clock denoted 25 minutes to 10."The writing was by now on the wall. The rep ort of June 1903 was damning: "The children are kindly taught and the teacher does her best, but the work of instructing a mixed school and infant class is hard for anyone and is becoming too much for Mrs. Foster, who should have permanent help. The staff should be strengthened without further delay". The inspector goes on to list the school's failings in reading, writing and arithmetic. No physical training is given, in contradiction to regulations. He recommends that the "Higher Principal Grant"should be awarded, but does so "with great hesitation". By November, however, things had reached crisis point.

"The mistress works under exceptional disadvantages. The school, (a very remote and isolated one), is ill- equipped with material necessary to carry it on properly, and also poorly staffed, Mrs. Foster needing the help of at least a paid monitress. The school at present fails to satisfy Article 85(a) of the Code, and the managers' attention is called to this serious fact. Indeed, the school is evidently being neglected by the Authorities at present".

Two weeks later, on November 20th 1903. Mrs. Foster sent in her Resignation, giving three months' notice.

Chapter 12
A Century of Change

Any investigation into the lives of our predecessors must resort at some stage to information from the tombstones in a graveyard. Clustered around Newlands Chapel now, at the beginning of the twenty-first century, are just a few dozen stones and slates, many of them memorials to twentieth century residents. Amongst them, however, rest some of those Chapel Wardens and farmers we have already met. So before we rush on to modern-day Newlands, we can spend some last moments remembering them. To help in our detective work, a plan of the graveyard as it was in 1950, before extensive "tidying-up", still exists with the old burial book.

To trace its history, we jump back again to the time of the Rev. George Tandy. Before 1863, all corpses had to be taken to St. Kentigern's churchyard in Crosthwaite, a somewhat undignified, bumpy ride. In the January of that year, a meeting was called under Tandy's leadership, "to take into consideration the best means of putting the Chapelgarth into such condition as may be requisite before applying to the Bishop to consecrate it as a burial ground".

Above: Newlands Churchyard, a place of rest for ancient families.

For this to happen, trenches needed to be dug to drain the land, and a higher wall had to be built. Over the next two years these improvements were carried out, with costs of 7s.9d paid out for the new gate, 10s.4d for gate irons and stoops, and 3s.0d for walling. With the help of a voluntary collection in the church, these and the subsequent costs of a Pall (17s.2d) and a Bier (10s.) were almost met by 1869. In that year, however, the wardens resorted again to a rate of 2d. in the pound "to be levied in the vale to meet such expenses as are lawfully chargeable to the Church rate". Then, as now, not everyone was happy! The following year we learn that the 2d. rate had been collected from all except John Hodgson of Littletown who refused to pay his 9s.1d.

Nevertheless, by then a Sexton had been appointed, in the shape of William Hodgson of Akin, (perhaps his relative John had wanted the post?) and presumably the burial ground was in business. Disappointingly, there is no mention of a "grand opening"with the first burial. This took place on, of all days, December 25th, 1869! The unfortunate star of the show was Mary Fisher of Low Houses, aged 83 years. Special thanks "for his onerous services"were recorded to the churchwarden John Wilson who seems to have taken on the role of treasurer over these difficult years. Their problems were not yet over, as in 1870 the chapel suffered a burglary, causing 19s. worth of damage as well, and it was found that the burial ground needed extra draining. "It was proposed by J M Hayton and seconded by Thomas Hodgson that the inhabitants of Newlands each give a day's labour towards completing the same, in lieu of charging the expenses upon the church rate". John Hodgson continued his refusal to pay up, even though at only 1d in the pound in 1870, he owed only 4s.6d. Presumably he also declined the suggestion of contributing a day's labour. (He must also have taken himself off somewhere else to be buried, as there is no entry for him in the official Burial book!)

The unfortunate Rev. Tandy had not been able to stay at Newlands long enough to see the completion of his project, which was carried on by the Rev. Rutherford. But it is fitting that one of the tombstones still standing reads, very simply, "Jesu, Mercy, GEORGE MERCER TANDY, priest, born August 6th. 1819, died May 25th. 1897." Moses Mawson of Emerald Bank, who had served the community so faithfully, unfortunately died, at the age of 85, in 1868, before all the preparations were completed, so was buried at Crosthwaite. But the family tomb is there, round the east side of the chapel, with the date of his wife Sarah's death in 1892, and some fascinating information about their sons, Moses and Peter, who died far from their roots, in Australia and New Zealand. These were the days of speculation, world-travel and exploration. A new life with unlimited land to farm, or minerals to discover, must have seemed an exciting challenge to young men looking for an escape from the centuries-old ways of the Newlands Valley.

Nearby, on another stone we learn even more of the fate of the Mawson dynasty: Their son Abraham also died in Australia, in 1900, whilst daughters Esther and Maria never married, and later moved into Keswick. The name of Mawson, once so proudly represented, disappeared from the Valley with the death of daughter Martha in 1903. Very close to old Moses Mawson lies his brother-in-law and friend, John Dover, who died at Lowhouses in 1886, but sadly

Moses Dover and family lie buried outside the chapel door.

without his wife Jane who is remembered on the stone, but who was interred at Crosthwaite many years earlier. Standing tall and proud outside the Chapel entrance porch, is the family tombstone of their son, Moses Dover of High Snab, who died in 1918, three hundred and forty four years after his ancestor William arrived at the same farm from Bassenthwaite! Again, the headstone tells a sad tale. Moses' wife Ann and his son Joseph both died before him, and they had lost two young sons in childhood. Only their daughters Jane Ann and Elizabeth survived well into the nineteen hundreds. Yet another family was destined to fade out of Newlands, with both daughters remaining unmarried.

The old Burial Book, recording all interments since 1869, tells of many husbands, wives and children whose remains lie deep in the turf in the Chapel Graveyard, but whose memorial stones have long since succumbed to the ravages of Lakeland wind and rain. But others stand there still, reminding us of Peter and Elizabeth (Betty) Wren, several generations of Joseph Wrens,

John and Fisher Thwaite, and, on a headstone near the porch, of William Hodgson, the first Sexton, who died at "Aitken"on September10th. 1897, buried alongside so many of his late friends.

We should not leave the nineteenth century without a further look at what was, after all, the most important aspect of these men's lives, their farming. Although sheep were by far the most important animals on the farms, cattle played their part too. In a remarkable old leather-bound diary written by the farmers John Thwaite and his son Fisher Thwaite over a period covering 1770s to 1850s, we read of the "appointments"kept by the bulls of the valley as they "served"the cows. The writing is at times elegant and clear; the spelling, however, is somewhat phonetic. To read the names aloud is to hear again the long, rolling vowels of this ancient dialect. The bulls seemed to have the pleasure of duty at various farms. The "Read (red) coowe", the Brandy Cow, the Donney (Dun?) Cow and the Broken Horn Cow all get their turn. A fearful remedy for any "Hoolish cattle"is prescribed as follows:

"3oz. of salt Petter

1 oz. of Roashallam

1 oz. of Boalalienock

2 oz. of Bliew Vitral.

Boil in a Quart watter to three Gils or one pint down."

The entries in the little book are by no means chronological. Spaces are filled in at later dates, notes are added upside down and scribblings understood by only the writer leave us intrigued. None more so than the cryptic notes on the first pages: "October the 9th 1770.

Sent to Daniel Fisher £3-3s to pay to Ann Carter 3s per weke.

Sent to Elizth. Scott 3s-0. and to Joseph Rowling 1s-0.

Treated Daniel Fisher with three quarts of Ale for his troble conserning Ann Carter".

Further expenses are incurred regarding Elizabeth Scott:

"Werent"(Warrant?) 2s-6d

Ale 2s-0d

Ale 4s-0d

To Constable (!) 1s-0d."

We are left wondering what they had been up to!

More mundane events are also carefully recorded. Occasionally there is a list of those who paid rent to the lord of the manor, from which we learn who was living where, and the amounts paid. Each year, one responsible individual had the probably unpopular task of collecting the "Lord's Rent", and John Thwaite lists them all from 1791 to 1812. We also get a glimpse of the work on their fields and meadows, with cart-loads of lime frequently bought from John Walker, and bushels of Barley and Oats sold to various neighbours. A few entries tell of basic food supplies: butter (6 pounds at 1shilling a pound), "chese"bought from Robert Bell, malt and hops from Moses Mawson, and potatoes from Wilson Tyson. A household "shopping list"in the early 1800s included one stone of "flower", a pound of sugar, the luxury of a pound of tea, and the ever-necessary pounds of candles. Every now and then, John Mumberson would be paid for supplying "beaf"and veal, usually washed down with ale. Brandy is ordered occasionally, while we are left to wonder what was the effect of this potent mixture: "3 Pennyworth Spirit of Camphire, 3 Pennyworth of Lodanum to a glass of best Rum."

John and Fisher Thwaite tried to keep an accurate account of all sorts of monetary transactions. On one occasion, however, things seem to have got into a muddle: "November 15. 1823. A Memorandam made betwixt John Fidler and Fisher Thwaite of the Chapel Money. I gave him 4 guineas, and the rest to him, 8 shillings and 11d, but he gave to me 6s-6d, and then I laid down 5 for you for your Sheir, and their was a day of threshing besides which I think I must charge 2s-6 to you"! John Fidler is an enigma. The surname occurs only for this brief period in the Valley. In July 1823 his cow had been served by the Bull. A check with the Chapel Wardens' Accounts shows that he was a Chapel Warden in 1822, representing "Howe's tenement", with John Thwaite, (Clark's tenement) succeeding him the following year. We never hear of him again.

The only other mention of Guineas in the notebook, is near the beginning, when John Thwaite meticulously copies out details of the Weight of a Guinea, from before the first year of the reign of George 3rd, (1760), through to its weight in 1772, concluding , "The foull weight of a guinea: 5. 9grams."

Dotted throughout the pages are references to the Thwaites' flocks of sheep. In 1822 John had 108 Yews, 70 Wethers, (males), 64 Hogs (one year-olds), and 54 Lambs. This flock of around 300 was fairly typical of the average Newlands farmer. Almost all of the men mentioned in the diary were owners or tenants of the scattered fellside farms.

Year by year, they continued the age-old tradition of sheep-farming: lambing, clipping, fighting diseases in their flocks, battling with the winter snows and trying to find a market for their wool. Canon Rawnsley, an astute observer of rural life, writing in 1911, gives us this account of the battle against diseases: "The maggot-fly is not the only plague that troubles our mountain sheep, for the fluke in the liver is a common complaint, sheep-rot is another, and last and most curious is a disease that is called "sturdy". The shepherds who are Norsemen do not know that when they say a sheep is "sturdy"they are talking Norman-French, but so it is, for the word "etourdi", meaning giddy, exactly describes the condition of the sheep in whose brain this living torment is growing". ("By Fell and Dale at the Lake District.")

By 1900, very few still depended on the essentially upland breed of Herdwick sheep, so recognisable still today with the black wool of the lambs, the stocky legs and smiling faces. Way back in 1787, James Clark , in his Survey of the Lakes, had quoted various tales and traditions associated with these animals, including the myth that "they are seen before a storm, especially of snow, to ascend against the coming blast and to take the stormy side of the mountain, which saves them from being overblown", to which Peter Crosthwaite, the Keswick Museum Owner, had responded with, "O, for Shame, Mr. Author! neither the present generation nor their forefathers before them ever knew Cumbrian Sheep keep the weather side of a mountain in a storm when they could get to the leeward."It remains true, however, that the Herdwicks can withstand being buried in snow for several days, living off their own fat, and even perhaps sucking oil out of their wool. And most amazing of all, is the way in which a Herdwick instinctively stays on its own "heaf", the pasture where it was weaned.

These tough little animals had been gradually improved over the centuries, so that, by 1879, John Wilson who was farming with a large flock of Herdwicks high up at Keskadale, could write with great pride and obvious love of the breed. That year saw the publication of a new edition of the "Shepherds' Guide", which for generations was the "bible"of flockmasters and farmers, declaring almost legally what were the distinctive markings on sheep belonging to individual owners. The original "Guide"for the Western fells was produced by J. Walker of Martindale in 1817. The writer of the New Guide of 1879, Daniel Gates, had requested information from local farmers about the essential qualities to look for in the judging of Herdwick sheep. Several letters were printed at the end of the tome, including one from John Wilson and his cousin Edward Nelson of Gatesgarth. Although rather lengthy, it is worth reading almost in full for the vivid descriptions that seem to bring the animals to life.

"Dear Sir, It is above all things necessary that a Herdwick should have a good coat; this should be long and well-knit, of good broad wool, which should grow out well to the extremeties; a good "toppin"is also much admired, and this shows that the animal is likely to grow a good fleece. A Herdwick cannot thrive well in winter with a thin coat, as in such case it is unable to withstand the inclemency of the weather. A good crop of wool also adds much to the receipts of the flockmaster. The head is one of the next points of importance. This should be strong and broad with an arched nose, which is expressive of boldness and courage; it should be wide and open at the muzzle, with a deep jaw; the latter of these points denotes strength. A pair of nice horns add largely to the appearance of the male animal, though they are not desirable in the female; they should be of whitish colour, smooth and well-turned, not too small or too wide, and rising well out of the back of the head. A good, prominent eye is important, improving the appearance of the sheep. The ears should be white and sharp and stand up well, as any tendency to droop betokes a want of spirit to grapple with hill life. In colour the head should be light grey, with a hoarfrost nose, a rustiness about the poll, as well as a lion-like mane. These are all solid requirements. The body should be shaped like a barrel, the legs well to the outside; a broad breast, placed forward, as the forequarters are chiefly relied on both for constitution and the scales. The knees should be strong, and the bone thin to fetlock; and then a big white foot to follow. The hind legs to spring from a well-muttoned thigh, thin shaped with plenty of bristles, looking rather upwards. The tail to reach no further down than the camerals, and thick at the root. A sheep should be well ribbed up, the greater their power to endure hunger; the back broad and well filled in behind the shoulders, when turned up to have a deep and broad breast, with soft, kindly wool upon it, showing a natural propensity to grow wool..............The Herdwick which was formerly an ill-developed, coarse-wooled animal, is now well formed, and in place of the "hempen locks", is now covered with good wool, which is eagerly sought after by local manufac-turers . . . . As requested by you, we have given the foregoing as a result of our united practical experience.

With best wishes for the success of your "Shepherds' Guide",

We remain, yours truly, Edward Nelson (Gatesgarth)

John Wilson (Keskadale)".

And so we come to the Shepherds' Guide itself. Between its covers lay carefully recorded details of the way in which sheep belonging to every farmer in Cumberland and Westmorland were marked for identification. The system involved a complicated series of "lug"marks. Any northern parent threatening their offspring with "a clip round the lugs"is unwittingly referring to the old Norse/Cumbrian practice of clipping variously shaped notches and

JOHN WILSON, Keskadale. Dale Stock—Square forked far, under key bitted near; stroke over and down both shoulders, W on near side. Twinters, red on head. Wethers, black.

Steel Side Stock Square forked near, under key bitted far, wool marks some as above.

Aikin Brow Stock Cropped and under key bitted near, upper fold bitted far, stroke down near buttock, W on near side. Wethers and Twinters distinguished as above

WILLIAM HODGSON, Aikin; under halved both, blue pop on top of shoulders.

JOHN THWAITE, Gillbrow; cropped near, upper key bitted far, stroke across fillets, black pop on back.

JOHN DOVER, Birkrigg; cropped far, under halved near, stroke near shoulders, pop on back.

Pages from the 'New Gates Shepherds Guide' of 1879. Lug marks and smit marks handed down through generations of Newlands' farmers.

slits into the ears of the sheep. The word lug did not originally mean ear, but was derived from the Norse log, meaning law, thus giving the ear notches a legal recognition in establishing ownership. The outcome of generations of this practice resulted in the hundreds of pictures in The Shepherds' Guide, showing the lug marks and the daubed "smit"marks of all flocks. There we find our John Wilson of Keskadale, whose Dale Stock are marked thus: "Square forked far, under bitten near; stroke over and down both shoulders; "W"on near side. Twinters, red on head. Wethers, black."His Aikin Brow stock are "cropped and under key bitted near, upper fold bitted far, stroke down near buttock, "W"on near side."(Got the idea??) Perhaps the illustration will help, with the sheep not only of John Wilson, but also of William Hodgson of Aikin, (the sexton), John Thwaite of Gillbrow and John Dover of Birkrigg.

Also recorded in the New Shepherds' Guide, are the marks of sheep belonging to the Graves brothers. With claims of Newlands forefathers way back in the 14th century, and a direct line of descent from a Reuben Grave farming at Skelgill in the 1660s, there was now another Reuben, farming at Low Snab, in 1881. In 1830, at the age of 21, he had declared at the christening of his cousin Grace Thwaite that he would wait to marry her. This he had done, in June 1857! Also farming in Newlands in 1881, at Gillbank and back at the family seat of Low Skelgill, were his unmarried brothers Simeon and Levi, with sister Mary. (Mollie Lefebure, in her book "Cumberland Heritage"has traced the Skelgill connections of the family through the generations, and Mr. Eddie Taylor has produced an extensive genealogical survey of all the Graves up to the present day). The Graves were continuing the traditional ways of farming still widespread throughout the Valley.

Another important part of Newlands life, however, was unfolding during these years down in the heart of the valley, at Stair. For centuries there had been at least two mills in this vicinity. Ten-year leases were granted way back in the 1500s to local farmers who worked the corn and flour mills, while weaving, carding and spinning of wool was carried on in individual farmhouses, mainly by the women and children. But the Industrial revolution, changing life all over the country, brought large, mechanised factories even into these remote corners. The old corn/flour mill on the banks below Stoneycroft changed hands several times during the mid-eighteen hundreds, until industrialisation brought the inevitable closure. An article in the "Carlisle Journal"of March 1886 spells out the looming threat. "A great change has come over the flour-mill trade of the district. Year by year the small mills, picturesquely situated in the country, upon the banks of limpid(?) streams, are one after another becoming untenanted or disappearing altogether, and the miller, as hero of romance or the subject of poetic description, is heard of no more. The miller's "moulter dish", with which he used to take pay in kind for his service when he ground wheat or oats for a farmer, may now be sent to a local museum."

The woollen mill by the bridge flourished for some time. Men and women had been employed there since the early years of the century. Parish baptismal records show that in 1808, Joseph Tindal, a "woollen manufac-turer", had taken up residence with his wife and family. He was joined in 1810 by Robert Proddow, then by Jeremiah Pearson, and Thomas Woof, all with their families. In the 1830s at least four other men were employed as weavers, spinners or carders at Stair Mill.The 1841 census listsHenry Holmes, 60, a wool carder, Thomas Robinson, 40, a weaver with his wife and nine children, and Thomas Martin, spinner, and his family. By 1851, at least five families gained a living from the Wool Mill. Among the wool-spinners, fullers and carders was Thomas Williamson, aged 48yrs, with his wife and seven children, six of whom were listed as "employed in the factory". Their ages ranged from 22 to 7. Only a four year old daughter and a two year old grand-daughter had not yet started work! These seemed to be thriving, busy times for the mill, yet ten years later, in the 1861 Census, there is no mention at all of the industry. We learn only of John McDowell the miller at the Corn Mill. The next census is equally uninformative about what was going on in the large old mill buildings. Only in 1891 do we find a clue, with the occupation of one Robert Graves stated as "Pencil Maker". The premises were being used for the grinding of plumbago, the lead for the well-established pencil manufacturing industry in Keswick.

By the end of the 1800s, life was in some ways returning to what it had been like some 80 years earlier. The activities in the mines had dwindled almost to a standstill by 1890, and as we have seen, the woollen mill was all but forgotten. What had been a significant influx of newcomers to work in these places had dwindled to just a few new families around the area. In nearby Braithwaite and Thornthwaite, with Force Crag and other mines continuing in operation much later, mining was a way of life. The 1891 Census in Newlands, however, reveals the continuation of local people farming the land. Some of the sons and daughters had left the valley for work industrial towns, to make fortunes abroad, or just to find employment in Keswick, but in many cases there had been at least one son left to carry on the work of his ancestors. Among the remaining "off-comers"in 1891, we find at Swinside a blacksmith and several lead-miners from Shropshire and from Cornwall, at Skelgill a mining engineer from Flintshire and at High Snab miners from Worthing and Montgomeryshire. The only other resident from any distance was the vicar, the Rev. Robert Armstrong, "Clerk in Holy Orders", who hailed from Scotland.

One farmer who had "diversified"by 1881 was John Cowman at the "Swinside Beer House". He was described in the census as a widower and farmer of 16 acres- not very many. But he had seen an opportunity to serve the needs of not only local people, but probably of the stream of miners trudging from the Keswick area to Newlands. At the end of the row of terraced cottages opposite the farm, John had set up his Beer House, where

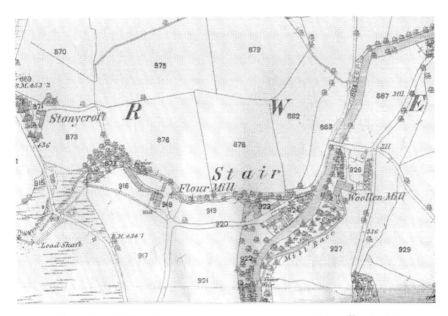

From the 1862 ordnance survey map, showing the mills at stair.

he remained for the next twenty years. By 1901, he had risen to the rank of "Innkeeper"at the "Swinside Inn". The need for a fairly "rough and ready"drinking hole as it would have been in the early days, perhaps arose from the up-market development of the old "Sportsman"Inn, across at Mill Dam. Since our last visit to this social centre of the Vale, when Henry and Jane Lowden had raised their large family there, the Inn had welcomed several different managers. An important change in its history took place around 1883. An Indenture of that year records a sale of "All that Customary Inn or Public House called The Sportsman Inn and the outhouses and garden situate at Mill Dam", involving 3 Revs. and Hon. Trustees, including Lord Leconfield, John Fisher Grave of Low Snab, and Joseph Tickell of High Lodore. Soon afterwards, a new building appeared in place of the old inn. Still standing today, over a hundred years on, but sadly under threat of demolition, the strangely out-of-place wooden residence, with the date 1888 over the door, was the new "Newlands Hotel". The first Hotel manager must have been Joseph Throughear. His death is recorded on the Chapel yard tombstone, with that spelling, in 1890, when he was living at the Newlands Hotel. (In the Whitehaven and Cockermouth areas, the "Trohear"family had

The Newlands Hotel in happier days.

run wines and spirits businesses and breweries in the 1870s.) A year later we read in the census that his widow, Sarah "Troughear", was "Hotel Keeper", living there with her daughter. The Hotel changed hands, and at the beginning of the twentieth century was in the care of George Bird and his wife.

The new establishment was very well situated to take advantage of the ever-increasing number of tourists at the turn of the century. The thrill of the Coach-and-horse "circular", from Keswick to Buttermere, was a "must"for anyone who could afford it. Way back in 1778, Thomas West had described these "upper regions"as "inaccessible to man". In Mannex and Whelan's 1847 Directory we read that "It is not quite so bad now as it was then, for a carriage road has since been made from Keswick through Newlands to Buttermere". The golden age of tourism had arrived. Day after day, processions of coaches, their horses sweating and steaming under the strain, wound their way uphill and downdale. "There is no better five shillings' worth of carriage driving at the Lakes than can be enjoyed by all who gather in the Keswick Market Place on a fine morning at ten o'clock, and take their seats on any of the char-a-bancs waiting to convey them up Borrowdale, over the Honister Pass to Buttermere, and thence home by the Newlands Vale to Keswick". The writer, possibly Canon Rawnsley, then makes a strangely "modern-day"request: "One thing we ask for, to ensure our pleasure, and that is that the smokers

Four-in-Hands negotiating the 'Devil's Elbow' below Keskadale farm, on the Buttermere - Newlands round.

153

Edwardian tourists on the bridge at Stair.

shall take a back seat." The narrative takes us through the day's journey, until, after a slow walk up from Buttermere, the Hause is reached and the travellers pass by Keskadale, "in its picturesque quaintness", whilst Aikin Knott and Bawd Hall stand in ruins. This, with a later reference to the graphite works at the old woollen mill in Stair, date the account just at the turn of the century.

Recently, Jeff Taylor of Keswick has recorded the personal memories of his mother, Lizzie, whose own father, Frank Richardson, was one of the drivers. "He was a four-in-hand driver, which meant he controlled four horses; it wasn't the easiest thing to do; some fellows could only manage two-in-hand, and others only a one-horse fly. . . . The coach left Keswick at ten o'clock in the morning and didn't get back 'til six o'clock in the evening . . . I used to go with him sometimes and I used to sit on the box-seat up front next to me father. When we were coming back over Newlands Hause, I remember looking down off the coach and seeing that the wheels were right on the edge of a tremendous drop. I don't know how they managed to stay on the road, mind; the horses seemed to know where to go. All the drivers used to tell stories; passengers used to ask them about the area and they used to make it all up.....One woman asked him why that mountain was called Catbells and he said that there was once an old woman who lived up there, and she was a witch and she had three cats who had bells round their necks. It didn't matter what he told them; they used to lap it up. All the drivers used to do it because they had to work for their tips. ....When they finished using horses and went on to charabancs, me father had to take his horses to Penrith Market to be sold and our Dick went with him. When they came back, our Dick said there were tears in me father's eyes at having to let them go".

The census at the end of the century saw many of the younger generations of old families on the farms: Thwaites and Graves (Skelgill), the Hodgsons and the Wrens (Littletown), the Dovers (High Snab), the Wilsons (Birkrigg) the Mawsons (Gill Brow) and the Clarks ("Rowlands House"). This last farm had for centuries been known as Low Houses, as it still was in the 1881 census. With another farm at "Low House"further up the vale in Littledale, there must have been much confusion. Families of Rawlings and Rowlings had lived in Newlands for generations, their residence frequently being "Low Houses". Very occasionally, there are references to a tenement at Rowling End, the name of the craggy fell above the houses. Perhaps somewhere in the past is a link between the family name and the mountain fell, but use of the house-name is difficult to follow. In the eighteen-eighties the Clark family were well-established at Low Houses, with the census indicating more than one dwelling house there. Living with Wilson Clark in one part of the farm, were his wife Martha Elizabeth and his 86yr. old father-in-law, John Dover, formerly of Birkrigg. On January 25th 1886, John died at the ripe old age of 91, and his burial registration recorded the place of death as "Rowland House". His tombstone, however, retains the name Low Houses. Five years later we have the first census recording of "Rowland House", replacing the old name. Over the next twenty years or so, we find variations such as "Rowland End"and "Rowling House", settling eventually on today's "Rowling End", the same as the fell-side.

By 1900, farm tracks were still muddy and rough, implements still basic, transport still horse-and-manpower, and many old customs still traditional. Life, as we have seen from the school records, was tough, cold and unsophisticated. The valley dwellers still, on the whole, knew little of life in the big cities. They had escaped the horror of grimy factories, disease-ridden slums and workhouses. The woollen-mill-cum-plumbago factory had brought a taste of industrialisation to Newlands, but the old mill building stood neglected and in a state of disrepair.

The opening of the twentieth century brought a dramatic change in the usage of the old mill buildings. The old workplace of weavers, carders and spinners and lead grinders was up for sale. The Rev. T. Arthur Leonard, a

Uncle Bill, diary writer, and friends at the Holiday Fellowship Centre.

congregational Minister from Colne, had an inspired vision. He had already organised basic, healthy, outdoor holidays in the fells for his Lancashire Mill-working parishioners. In his "Adventures in Holiday -Making"we read:

"When we heard that a certain old mill at Stair in the Vale of Newlands might be purchased cheap, we dreamt of its possibilities as a simple-life guest house.......It seemed ideal with a clear, swift-flowing beck in which to bathe, and the steep, beautiful fells standing close by. It seemed a heaven-sent gift for our crowds of nature-lovers. But the cautious ones on the committee thought otherwise, for they had received disparaging reports from others who had also visited the place."

Arthur Leonard did not give up. He brought some of the committee to see the mill.

"The day I led the inspection is one I am never likely to forget. It was November, and our prayers for a sunny day had not been answered. The train was late, we missed our lunch, the rain clouds hung low over the hills and the old mill with its dirty floors and general air of dilapidation would have depressed anybody but an inveterate optimist who had seen a sunny vision of its possibilities. So the deputation wandered around in glum silence and returned to Manchester to pass a unanimous recommendation to turn the scheme down".

Undaunted, T. Arthur Leonard eventually persuaded people to back his scheme, and was able to buy the building, which became The "Newlands Guest House". "We had converted the drab, dirty mill into a place of sweetness and light. We had pitch-pine partitions, raftered ceilings, cream-coloured walls and white-painted window frames. The old wheel was sold for a good sum. A larder took its place. The furnace room at the back where formerly the lead had been roasted, became the kitchen, and so it was the best-loved of all the centres".

Within three years it became a centre for the Cooperative Holidays Association, and later the Holiday Fellowship. Recently, Mrs. Celia Costello discovered a diary written around 1905 by her great-uncle, William Codling, poet, journalist and adventurer. In "Uncle Bill's Diary"we re-live the adventures of the enthusiastic young men and women who came to climb the hills purely for pleasure, an incomprehensible notion to previous generations of local farmers.

"SUNDAY: Awake at 6am. Get up (It's the solemn truth) and go for a plunge in the beck. After breakfast dress for church, but instead about 36 of us go for a walk on Causey Pike.

Commence to climb to the top.

Mist commences.

Commence to get tired.

Continue climbing.

Mist Continues.

Continue to get tired.

Sit down to look at each other and at our SUNDAY CLOTHES !!

More climb! More mist! More tired!

Give it up all except 6 who reach top."

Even more amazing than Uncle Bill's accounts, are his photographs. How, we wonder, could those unsuitably dressed visitors, especially the ladies, have scrambled up the rocky hillsides in their fashionable costumes? Millican Dalton, the eccentric adventurer, was to become a leader at the Holiday Fellowship, but for two years only, as he was too much of a maverick to fit in with the rules and regulations! The story of the old mill buildings continues up to this day, as we shall see later. But life in these early 1900s was about to change for both carefree holiday-makers and old farming families alike. Just ten years after "Uncle Bill's"adventure at Stair, he and his friends would be dragged into the horrors of the First World War.

THORNTHWAITE.
BRAITHWAITE.

PORTINSCALE.
NEWLANDS.

FOR THOSE SERVING IN HIS MAJESTY'S FORCES.

| VOL. 2. No. 2. | CANDLEMAS, 1940. | PRICE THREEPENCE. |

Chapter 13
Wartime in Newlands

On a wall of Newlands Chapel we find the sad evidence of the tragedies the War brought to Newlands: "Roll of Honour, Newlands School". After the resignation of Mrs. Jane Foster in 1903, several other teachers had continued the daily struggle in the tiny school. Not many of them could cope for long with the frustrations of failing supplies, extremes of weather, unhealthy conditions and the lively exuberance of infants interrupting the studies of the older children. We read in the Log-Book of children walking through shoulder-high snow, then taking all morning to dry off their soaking clothes in front of the fire. On one summer day the "distressed"children begged to go to the stream for water; on another there was such an "offensive"smell in the schoolroom that the teacher took them outside for lessons. Occasionally the teachers Amelia Barnes and Jane Fairly would take the children on long rambles, collecting frog-spawn, flowers and ferns. The pull of the outdoor life remained too strong for some of the lads when eight of them "ran away after the hounds". Inspectors continued to report that "changes of Teacher have retarded the recovery of this school". Notwithstanding, prize-giving days came around each year, with children from the Robinson, Grave, Atkinson, Thwaite and Edmondson families regularly doing well.

Above: David Imrie's sketch of Braithwaite for the heading of the Wartime Newsletter.

The Great War was to alter the lives of every one of these families. The "Roll of Honour"in the Chapel tells its sad tale: Joseph Watson, Daniel Watson, who in 1905 won school prizes for his work, but was also "kept in"for being cheeky; Cyril Thwaite who had gained a "perfect attendance"certificate in 1905; Robert Postlethwaite, whose sore foot kept him absent from school in 1904 because he had 2 ½ miles to walk there, also "killed in action"; Andrew Muncaster, who as a youngster "jumped from a wall and hurt his ankle"; George Grave, a new pupil in November 1906, George Bowe, John Edmondson, and George and Stanley Atkinson. Here we also find the names Lewthwaite and Robert Foster, (killed in action), the two sons of the former schoolmistress Jane Foster. Almost one hundred years later, we read this Roll of Honour and remember them.

In the years following the war, however, young people in Newlands and Keswick, as indeed all over the country, were bent on forgetting the horrors and enjoying themselves. The "Keswick Reminder"in April 1923 carried this announcement:

"The Newlands Valley Institute. A Grand Concert will be held at 7.30pm on Friday, March 9th to be followed by a Dance. Admission 2s. Supper at a reasonable charge. Music by Bowman's Band.

The "Queen of the Lakes"Char-a-banc will leave the Market Square, Keswick, at 7. 0pm."

Not everyone, however, was delighted by the news. The following week the newspaper carried another statement:

"The. Rev. E .H. F. May, Vicar of Newlands, begs to state that he has nothing whatever to do with the Concert and Dance advertised to take place on March 9th, 1923, at the wooden structure known as the "Newlands Institute". He is so constantly asked about the entertainments that take place in the building that he concludes that it is thought that he is the organiser. He is not. The building does not stand in Newlands Parish, but in Crosthwaite."Poor old vicar. Presumably everyone had a good time without him there!

Over the next few years, dances, concerts and fetes followed each other in rapid succession in various venues in and around Keswick. Even if the hard-working folk of the valley could not often participate in the dancing classes, evening classes and lantern lectures on offer, they surely did get to the Agricultural shows around the area, the Garden Fetes at Lingholm and their own local whist drives.

In an unexpected way, we find that at this time there was still a link with the centuries-old traditions of the Braithwaite area. The Medieval Manor

Court, referred to in much earlier chapters, was apparently still functioning! Its real practical value, however, was minimal, and it had continued simply because no-one had officially brought it to a close! So, in 1939, (we learn from the booklet published by the Womens' Institute in 1971), the very last "Court Leet"was held at the Royal Oak in Braithwaite. The Agent from Cockermouth Castle summoned the jurors, bailiffs and defenders. These, however, turned out to be very few in number. Mr. Herbert Barnes was Bailiff; the jurors, who were paid 10s. for their troubles, included Messrs. A. Wilson, J. Mossop and W. Burnett. "No Business"was recorded, and the meeting was followed by a traditional 2 course meal at the inn. Perhaps not the excuse, as had been in past times, for a hard night's drinking!

We learn from The Keswick Reminder that in February 1939, with tension mounting all over the country as Hitler threatened our safety, the local people threw themselves whole-heartedly into their annual Concert and Dance. This time, instead of a char-a-banc, a Bus was leaving the bus station for the rides to and from Keswick, and the music was provided by the "Gaiety Orchestra"; but otherwise the proceedings followed the usual pattern. The concert, entitled "Variety", was presented by Miss Ida Siddle and her pupils, assisted by Mr. Borthwick and party. The programme included a song and dance medley, a ventriloquist act, a tap dance, the Sleigh bells, a Dutch Interlude, "Rival Lovers"by Messrs. J. Brownlee and G. Fisher, and an impromptu monologue by the Vicar; no, not a change of heart by the Rev. May, but an offering from his successor, the popular Rev. Steele-Smith.

Mr. G .G. Grave was the M.C. The supper was given by the people of the Valley and was served by Mesdames Steele-Smith, W. Bainbridge, Robinson, Hind, Thwaites and Tyson.

A couple of months later, gas-masks were being distributed.

The "Keswick Reminder"over the following months records the mounting tension and the war-time restrictions that the people of Newlands experienced along with the outside world. Air-raid precautions were issued, air-raid Wardens were appointed, Black-out materials were advertised, food-rationing became part of every day life. In Keswick a "fags for the lads"fund was set up, and all over the area people got together to knit and sew and raise money to bring cheer to the troops. To keep up morale back at home, the Alhambra Cinema was showing Laurel and Hardy, Shirley Temple, Bulldog Drummond and "Owd Bob", while Gracie Fields was "Shipyard Sallie".

At the outbreak of the war, the "Braithwaite and District War Comfort Fund", with John Mossop Esq. of Sour Riggs in the Chair, had held its first meeting in the Schoolroom. In the next 3 years, £360 had been raised. The backbone of the scheme, according to the "Reminder", were the Cottage Whist Drives, where hostesses had raised anything from £5 to £20 in a single effort. An increasing number of men and women from Braithwaite, Thornthwaite and Newlands were joining the services. With 110 members of the fund knitting socks, pullovers and scarves, sending letters and postal orders, the sons of the area were kept as closely in touch as possible. In reply, by 1943, 382 letters, cables, airgraphs and postcards had arrived back home, all expressing great appreciation of the generosity of the people of Braithwaite and district.

After a space of twenty years, the "Above Derwent News-letter", for men serving in His Majesty's Forces, was re-born. During the First World War, this paper had been sent out to encourage the men far away from home, and in 1939 Braithwaite there still lived men who had been involved in that production. Once again, under a wonderful set of pseudonyms such as "Sleddergeggins", "Bogside", "Misfit"and "Barrowdores", they put pen to paper and produced over a dozen inspiring newsletters for the lads out on the battlefields. The editorial team, led by Mr. Anthony Wilson of Thornthwaite Mines, met at Stanger House, then owned by John Pearson, who supervised the village post office from that address. The editors of the first letter declared: "We think that at all costs, our men must not feel forgotten, that they must frequently be reminded of their people and homes", and they made a commitment to support and encourage "our men at the front, our workers in munition factories and those engaged in protecting our supplies". The chairman of the Parish Council, Mr. John Mossop, contributed his own encouragement, ending, "I am quite certain that Above-Derwent men, true Cumbrians, will maintain and uphold the traditions of the British Army, and when the time comes for you to return home, after winning the War, you are assured of a great welcome". Sadly, not everyone was to return for that welcome.

H.P. Haye, was given a special task in these early days of the war. In the December 1939 Newsletter, he tells the lads abroad: "It was one of my duties to go around Newlands seeking accommodation for mothers with young children. For the evacuees there was perfect safety amid beautiful surroundings, and I explained to their prospective hostesses that here was a chance of free help in the household, gratefully given. But those who were sent up to Newlands only managed to stick it for a few days. They thought it better to be dead in an air-raid than to be alive up here." In the first flush of the evacuation programme, Caleb Barnes, headmaster of Braithwaite School,

161

reported an increase of 77 children. By the Christmas, however, only 44 remained.

H.P.Haye's contributions to cheering on the local lads so far from home was often tongue-in cheek. In 1940 he had fun with the efforts of the district A.R.P. "It soon became evident that we must emulate the rabbit and be prepared to go underground at the first signs of danger. At first it was suggested that some disused mines up Newlands would provide an ideal bolting place for the people of this district, but from the first I distrusted this plan. Even if we did get warning of a raid before it actually occurred, by the time you got up and got dressed and made yourself a cup of hot tea and wandered all the way up. . . what I mean is that I'm not going up Newlands in a half dressed condition and with an empty stomach for all the ARP in the world; and besides, we ought to consider the people who live in Newlands. I know that in holiday season, when the visitors are with us, they are used to seeing strange sights come wandering up the vale, but the spectacle of the combined population of Braithwaite and Portinscale emerging from the chilly dawn wearing nothing but gas masks and nondescript articles of night attire might be more than they could stand, and I'm very pleased that those who control the A.R.P. in this district had the sagacity to discern the weak points of this suggestion."

Another regular contributor was "Sleddergeggins", whose fame was to spread world-wide through the pages of the Newsletter, as he entertained the "locals", but completely baffled their fellow service-men, with his broad-dialect ramblings. Here, we have room only for a short sample of his pithy observations, put together under the title "Screapins":

"Weel cawed Screapins twenty five 'ear sen an a booy oald scrat it was ta screap eneuf tagidder to write ta t'sowljers, an noo, cokswunters, ...anudder war brek out ta gi yan an excuse ta screap screapins tagidder ageann".

It used ta be t'fashun in t'Sooth African War to chrissen babbies sek neams as Redvers, Baden Powell an sek like. Sure eneuf t'fashun ull strike up ageann, an altho it's appen ower seun yit fer babbies, t'Kessick fwok hev mead a start an noo caw their Cooncillors sek neams as Hitler, Gobbles, Ribbintripe an sec like. Bit then, they allus was a gaumless lok o' yadderpets them Kessick Cooncillors, bit than ooar Coonncil is varra laal better, an t'next time thears an elecshun ah's gaan ta put up mesel"

"Ivverybody's thrang deuan their bit ageann just likke t'Boar War an t'last war, nut fergittan t'farmers. Eggs are thruppence aw riddy, milk's gone up a penny and they've aw bowt thersels a new pair o' yalla leggins on t'strength on't."

"Gammerstangs"was also a popular writer. He sent out snippets of "every-day"Braithwaite and Newlands life to remind the lads of home. By Easter 1940, he described how the men of the area were responding to the national "Dig and Plant"effort:

"Never has the home front been so busy with the plough as at present. Harry Walker of High Coledale is ploughing up-hill and down-dale at Blake Howe Hill, and young Banks Bowe has ploughed out Low Newlands field.....the same activity rules in Thornthwaite, Portinscale and Newlands. When the oats ripen, I hope we can get them ground at a local mill, and then I shall start eating porridge again."(To this day, it is possible to see the traces of wartime furrowing in dozens of fields around Braithwaite and up the Valley as high as Littledale.)

In the same edition, "Barrowdores"displayed her poetic talents. The lady hiding behind this pen-name, was Florence Taylor Robinson. Daughter of Nathan Robinson, the Postmaster living at the old Corn Mill in Stair, she continued to run the Post Office after him. Her seven verses on "Newlands in the Snow", after a particularly hard winter, may not have matched up to the lines of William Wordsworth, but must have brought many a smile to anxious and lonely young men in distant parts:

> "No doubt you have heard of the snow, lads,
> Which fell on the mountain side,
> And the fields and the lanes and the valleys
> Where peaceful folks reside.
> Have you heard how it cut folk off, lads,
> From the town and the pub and the kirk,
> And no-one got up in the mornings
> 'Cause no-one could get to work?

> And away up in Newlands Vale, lads,
> Where the Hivingsty winds its way,
> There were drifts that you couldn't see over,
> At least, so the farmers say.
> And one of them, when he looked up, lads,
> Gazes above and he shook his head,
> And he muttered "Ah'll be on't safe side",
> So he carried his spade to bed!

163

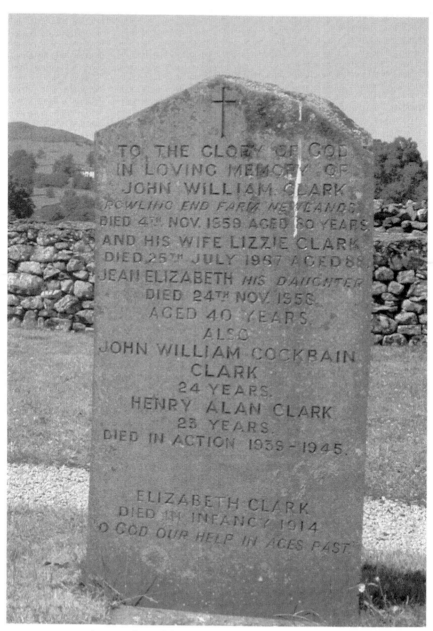

A reminder of the war years in the churchyard.

"Barrowdores" was to provide further light reading with "A Walk Round Newlands Valley"and "Haytime in Newlands", bringing memories of home to those so far away.

But, for all the entertainment value of the Above Derwent Newsletter, it served also a far more serious and often sad purpose. In its pages came news from the warfront, sometimes in the form of anecdotes and letters from sons abroad, but sometimes in unwelcome reports of missing or wounded soldiers and airmen, and ultimately of some deaths. In Newlands, one particular family was to mirror the hopes and aspirations, the triumphs and the tragedies, of so many others. Mr. and Mrs. John Clark of Rowling End Farm had three fine sons, all of whom were inspired by the prospect of flying for the Royal Air Force. The "Above Derwent Newsletter"of Summer 1940 reported that their eldest, Wilson Clark, was home safely after his experiences at Dunkirk. By 1942, this glowing tribute to the family appeared in the Newsletter:

"Mr. and Mrs. Clark of Rowling End Farm have good reason to be proud of their three air-minded sons. Wilson, the eldest, spent ten months in America, where he graduated as Sergt-Pilot. He returned to this country last month, and on account of his particular abilities was made Instructor of Flying. At the moment he is stationed not a hundred miles from home. An unexpected visit which he made to Rowling End the other weekend gave his people much pleasure. Although training the raw material how to fly seems less exciting than operational work, Wilson thinks that the latter is safer. He likes the States very much. John, the second son, is a Sergt-Oserver, and has been several times on operational flights over Germany. He is keen as mustard on his job. Alan, the youngest, expects to finish his training before Christmas, when he will be a Sgt-Wireless-Operator/Air-Gunner. We predict that Alan will be a really useful Air-Gunner. Despite the difference between flying and farming, they all give their father a hand with his work when they happen to be on leave. Well done, Rowling End!"

Tragically, only a few months later we read:

"We regret to have to record that John Clark is officially reported missing. Second son of Mr. and Mrs. Clark of Rowling End, John was a bomb-aimer, and it was while on a raid over Germany that his plane failed to return to base. We express our fervent hope that his anxious father and mother may soon have the best possible news of their grand lad."That news never came. Time dragged on, only for their grief to be increased beyond measure by the summer time: "Alan Clark has not returned from his first bombing raid over Germany. Alan was an air-gunner, and is the second of Mr. and Mrs. John Clark's three sons to be reported missing from a similar mission. No news has been received of his brother John, missing six months ago.....Wilson is at present home on leave".

Still standing in the churchyard in Newlands is the memorial stone to John William Clark, with his two sons, John William Cockbain Clark, and Henry Alan Clark, "who lost their lives while serving with the R.A.F."

One family name that has followed us through all the twists and turns of our Newlands story is "Thwaite". The 16th Century Thwaites of old "Keskadel"had moved around from farm to farm, married into most of the old Statesmen families and spread out and about in Borrowdale and Bassenthwaite. Still at Gillbrow farm when the New Gates' shepherds' guide was published in 1879, John Thwaite's sheep were "cropped near, upper key bitted far, stroke across fillets and black pop on back". An Edward Thwaites, (with the 's'), from Braithwaite, also had his sheep markings recorded in the guide. Little could either of them have envisaged the scene some sixty years later, when a crowd gathered sadly in the churchyard beneath the fells to witness the burial of Sgt. John Fisher Thwaite. The "Newsletter"records the day:

"It is with deep regret that we have to record the death of Sgt. John Fisher Thwaite. He was killed on the night of Oct. 22-23, when his plane crashed while on manoeuvres. He was 22 years of age. He was a fine type of young Englishman - six feet two inches in height and popular with all who knew him".

He had flown over Braithwaite just a few nights earlier, and wrote to his father saying he hoped he hadn't disturbed his sleep! The writer tells of the many sympathisers who had made the journey on foot to pay their last tributes, of the coffin draped with the Union Jack, and the service conducted by the Rev. Steele-Smith and the Rev. H. Crossland.

"He was laid to rest beside his mother in the peaceful valley of Newlands on a lovely October day. We extend our sympathy to his father Mr. Fisher Thwaite, who left the Newlands Valley many years ago for Australia, where he became a successful sheep-farmer, returning to the scenes of his youth on his retirement - and to his brother Bill."

The grief of old Fisher Thwaite is unimaginable: only four years before this tragedy, he had stood in the same churchyard on a cold March day, at the burial of Agnes, his wife, aged only 55. Even his years in Australia had ended with sadness, with the sudden death of his first wife just twelve days before they were due to return to England. Now, at the age of 82, he had lost one of his only two sons.

Far happier reading for the residents of Above Derwent were the letters from sons making the most of their experiences abroad, sometimes recounting amazing coincidental meetings, and otherwise just looking on the positive side of life. Billy Brocklebank wrote to his wife, "I was at the counter when a voice behind me shouted 'Wat's thoo deun here, hoo ista?' You could have knocked me down with a tractor! I spun round and discovered Frank Swainson; he had come on a message to our camp. We had a cup of tea and a crack; it was good to see him."Both Billy and Frank featured in the pages of the Keswick Reminder too, with their news from afar. Billy, (perhaps patiently awaiting the arrival of some promised knitwear ?), declared "Cush, it mun be a fair lang stocking", while Frank admitted, "It is nice to know we are not forgotten. I'm sure I'm no hand at writing letters of this sort. I can manage love letters best."

C.Q.M.S Alan Litt, from an old Gutherscale and Braithwaite family, wrote: "I am at present sitting under a fig tree, but the fruit is not quite ripe, so I am waiting patiently", and on another occasion described how a nine chickens' eggs hatched out in a truck as they were bumping around the desert.

In the February of 1943 the Newlands Valley representative of the W.V.S Cockermouth Rural Branch, assisted by friends and supporters, organised a Rummage Sale at Emerald Bank, and with donations and sundry sums made £17. 8. 6 for the Red Cross POW fund. On the 12th of that month news came through of a Newlands POW: "Regimental QSM George Vincent Turner of the Royal yank Corps, missing since the fall of Tobruk, is a prisoner of war in Italy. His mother, who lives at Newlands Vicarage, has just received a postcard from him saying he is well".

In the summer of 1943, a massive effort was organised in Keswick towards the national "Wings for Victory"scheme. The target given to Keswick, to be raised for provision of weapons and machinery, was £80,000. Every street, school, WI Group etc. in the town and surrounding villages was allocated a "mini-target"towards something specific. The children of Newlands school, under Miss Armstrong, were asked to contribute £45 for machine guns. By June, Keswickians had surpassed their target and their enthusiastic newspaper was declaring "Let's make it £120,000! (3 Bananas given by Mr. and Mrs. Marley of the Bank Tavern had been auctioned for £51. 7 6 at the WVS Military Whist Drive!) The final total was a magnificent £126, 236. 14s. 8d, which included £807. 0. 0. from the Newlands valley. In the "Reminder"of December 1943, we read of the "Newlands Efforts for Prisoners of War". "A whist drive, rummage sale and tea organised by the WVS resulted in £35. 16. 0 raised by the Newlands Dalesfolk for the POW fund. The Whist was in the Institute, the Sale and Tea at Emerald Bank, the home of the Misses Frost. Mr. G. G. Grave was M.C. at the Whist Drive, and the prizes were presented by Mrs. T Barnes of Uzzicar, described at 77 years of age as the youngest "lassie"in the room. Prizes were won by Mr. Bean (Swinside), Mrs. Litt-Wilson, Miss Wormersley, Mrs. Beatty (Birkrigg). Doll competition: given and dressed by Miss Hilda Johnson, won by Mr. Tingle. Stalls at the Rummage, Misses Frost, Mrs. J. Clark, Mrs. Wood, Mrs. Steele-Smith. Teas: Mrs. J. Folder, Mrs. J. Robinson, Mrs J. Clark, Miss Gibson and Miss Gladys Menhams of Rigg Beck. The donor of the cake was Mrs. Beatty."

Mrs. Litt-Wilson is still remembered by the present owners of Gutherscale, where she used to live. With her husband away in the services, she prepared herself for any unwelcome visitor at her lonely farmhouse, (or perhaps for German invaders?) by keeping a shotgun under her pillow! Gutherscale is tucked way out of sight, below the rocky track to Catbells, an oasis of tranquility; but we remember that way back in the 1660s, Cuthbert Gaskarth (of "Gutterskell") was being a nuisance to his neighbours by enclosing his land and stopping them from getting to market in Keswick! Some 150 years later, another Gutherscale owner made his mark in the valley by being the first to own a motor car.

Mrs. Steele-Smith, the Vicar's wife, was another of those ladies helping at the 1943 Rummage Sale. The previous year the wedding of her daughter Isobel to Thomas Standing had brought cause for celebration during the dark years, but soon afterwards, in April 1944, the Rev. Steele-Smith, "a most popular and beloved priest", left the Valley to take up a position in Bolton, Westmorland. He was greatly missed: "At Newlands he has been active in everything connected with the Valley, a friend to all and a friend indeed to those in need". His kindness and concern had stretched far beyond the narrow Vale of Newlands. A man of great academic achievment, an educationalist counting amongst former pupils Hastings Banda, who became president of Malawi, he was also working secretly in the support network for Jewish refugees.

To return to the "Above Derwent Newsletter"; one of the anonymous writers went by the strange name of "Oganach". Readers might well have detected the Highland resonance of the name, as the author of the chatty articles about local characters was David Imrie, the Scottish Gamekeeper at Lingholme. David had drawn the sketch used at the head of the Newsletter, depicting the village from the front of Scotgate farmhouse. His talents, however, extended beyond artwork to poetry and music, all inspired by his great love of the open air, the fells and the simple life. Living in an unsophisticated, basic hut in the woodlands on the lower Barrow slopes, he loved to wander up the fellside on a fine evening, to station himself high above the village and play his Scottish pipes, often with melodies he himself had composed.

Many years later, David was to describe one Saturday morning at the height of the War. He and another gamekeeper heard the erratic sound of a plane in trouble among the low cloud veiling the upper parts of Newlands. There was a crash and a silence. Realising that the plane had come down in the Little Braithwaite Wood, very near to David's hut, they hurried there, to find the police already on the scene, "beside a shattered Oxford Trainer, which had descended with such force that several larch trees were snapped off. Despite the strong smell of petrol, some spectators were smoking cigarettes. Inspector Bell of Keswick stopped that criminal carelessness. Quite soon he had the wreckage surrounded by police, who kept back sightseers, and in the afternoon they were augmented by soldiers from the D & M School at Portinscale."The crew of three had been killed. "On another occasion of low cloud", David wrote, in the 1971 W.I. publication on the village, "a plane, possibly a Spitfire, crashed into Scar Crags above Rigg Beck Ghyll. Only one man was involved, and he had been killed instantly. Some local men who were in the Home Guard manage to retrieve usable ammunition when the salvage men had finished. They did not take everything, because of the difficult situation, and some of the engine may still be seen in Rigg Beck".

And so the War years drew to a close. Life in many of the upper-valley farms had gone on relatively unchanged. Lambs continued to be born; clipping, dipping and marking was necessary every year; hay had to be mown and, with no electricity yet in the valley, peat or bracken had to be gathered in for fuel. The children made their arduous way on foot to the little school, they heard of the atrocities of the War, they knew that brave men from lower in the Valley had been killed in the conflicts, but their own lives were hardly changed.

Chapter 14
A Stroll around Newlands Today.

The Newlands Institute, scene of those lively dances, celebrations and concerts of half a century ago, is still there, in Stair, a hundred yards or so from the old woollen mill. But today, on a stroll through the village, we search in vain for other signs of the mid-1900s. A few hundred yards up the hill, on the site of the old corn mill, the 1901 census shows a post-office. Nathan Taylor Robinson from Borrowdale had married Grace Thwaite, daughter of John and grand-daughter of Fisher Thwaite, the diary writer of chapter 12! Nathan continued his trade as joiner and cartwright in addition to running the postal services. He was assisted by his son, Fisher Thwaite Robinson. aged 14, and recorded in the census as "post office messenger". (The distinctive name lived on!) Fisher's grandson, the present owner of the old corn mill, tells of the days when the young messenger had to set out on his push-bike to struggle over the Hause to Buttermere with a telegram, only to find on his return that there was another one to be delivered. He was paid 6d a trip for his troubles. In later years, Fisher carried on the joinery business,

Above: Millstone outside the old Corn Mill, Stair.

and delighted their friends and neighbours by clearing enough space in the store for merry evenings of dancing to the music of his fiddle. His sister Florence became post-mistress, while his younger brother Jack was the valley's first taxi driver and general handyman. During the First World War Jack was reported missing, presumed dead. Letters of condolence arrived. But Jack had in reality been shut off from communications in a Russian POW camp, and eventually returned safely to Newlands, where he and his wife Annie lived in the newly built Ellas Crag.

Many who still tramp the fells today will remember another feature of Stair hamlet, the shop and tea-room opposite Stair House. In 1964, the "Cumbria"magazine carried a special feature on personalities of the Vale of Newlands, with a photograph of Miss Sheila Brooks, who had converted part of the old Stair Farm barn for the shop. (Miss Brooks and her sister Moira had, before that, run the elegant old house at Emerald Bank as a private hotel). Today, the shop has disappeared and the barn has been split into several different homes. Across the road, the old Stair Farmhouse has recently been carefully renovated, with the old lintel above the door still reminding us of the mysterious possibility of a Fairfax connection. Leaving Stair, we walk up the valley towards Littletown. En route we pass Gillbank, once the home of "T'auld lord"John Fisher. What would he have made of the holiday cottages now replacing the farm, with the old barns refurbished as a private dwelling?

Beyond Gillbank is "Yewthwaite", which was for many years the "New"Vicarage. Built near the turn of the century, the first occupants were the Revd. Benjamin L. Carr, his wife Alice and their one year old daughter Lucie, who was to be immortalised in Beatrix Potter's "Tale of Mrs. Tiggywinkle."A succession of vicars and their families led eventually to the Revd. Steele-Smith's years of service during the war. By that time major renovations were needed, not the least of which is reflected in the vicar's requests for a new bath! Plaster was falling off the walls, the front room was damp and the chimneystacks were unsafe. Repairs were affected, and his daughter, the schoolteacher Isabel Standing continued to live there with her husband and children. She, too, was featured in the 1964 "Cumbria"interviews. Mrs. Standing kept the little school going during its last few years, while her husband Tom, a churchwarden, served as an ambulance driver. With his vehicle stationed at the garage in High Hill in Keswick, he had to drive his own car to Keswick before even setting out on any weekend or night-time emergency! Today, although part of the vicarage is let as holiday property, the family still maintain their connections with the Valley.

Beyond Yewthwaite is the huddle of dwellings at Littletown. Here we have a cameo of almost all aspects of Newlands life, past and present. The original vicarage, or, according to the 1862 map, the "parsonage", is perched on the hillside to the left. Above a doorway is a lintel with the engraving "Revd. J. M. AD 1811". The Rev. John Monkhouse is certainly credited with extending the original primitive living area, but the date, is something of a mystery, as he did not come to Newlands until 1840! Standing beside the vicarage, Croft House and Catbells Cottage occupy the site of the oldest Littletown farm, but are now private residences, with other outbuildings transformed into Causey Pike Cottage. Across the road at today's Littletown farm, traditional farming is combined with guest accommodation and restaurant facilities, with the addition of a brand new family house, fittingly built in traditional old style.

The family now at the farm tell the story of the previous generation, in the days of old Joseph Wren. As owner of all three buildings in the Littletown group, he decided in 1911 to move out of one and into part of the old Vicarage, necessitating an "all change"by the other families. On the appointed morning, everyone made great efforts to pack trunks and boxes, collect kitchen equipment and turn out for the move, only to discover old Joseph still asleep in bed!

There are still those at the farm who remember the family's war contributions. The Swainsons had moved in at the beginning of the century, and one of their daughters, now Mrs. Relph, tells of her father's involvement with the Home Guard. With his colleagues, Maurice drove an army truck, exempt from the petrol restrictions, over to Thirlmere to "guard the dam"! While we might wonder just what this handful of countrymen could have achieved faced with a barrage of German bombs, an interesting story throws light on the situation. Recently, a Mr. D. Whitfield from Darlington, wrote to the local "Keswick Reminder"with an account of an escapade in 1943. He and a schoolfriend, Youth Hostelling in the area, explored the dam and descended one of the drain shafts. Upon clambering out, they were confronted by the Keswick Home guard, rifles at the ready. "It took about half an hour to convince the officer in charge that we were merely two English schoolboys, not German Paratroopers or saboteurs sent in to blow up the dam".

The Relphs also remember how the motor-cyclists from the M&D camp at Portinscale would drive their machines across the fields and up the old miners' tracks. As part of their training, they had to submerge the bikes in the beck, then know how to start up the waterlogged vehicles again. Bren Gun carriers also traversed the farmers' fields, negotiating the rough terrain up to the old Dalehead mines.

During all of these troubled years, farming continued much as before. Mrs. Relph's Uncle, Eardley Swainson, was also interviewed for the 1964 article in the "Cumbria"magazine. As most of these remote farms did not acquire cars or tractors until the 1940s or 50s, he well recalled his younger days when, with horse and cart, he used to collect the coals from Braithwaite railway station, and a ten shilling note would buy 10 or 11 cwt. of coal and leave him with a little much-needed change. On the farm they would get up at 3am in summer to gather the sheep. "The pace of life has quickened. Now (1964) it's all of a splutter". At haytime too, the day would begin with the horses in the fields at three in the morning, so that they could avoid the "heat of the day". (Perhaps summers were better then?) Eardley even remembered the days before tarmac arrived in the valley, when the tracks were covered with broken stone "with a bit of earth thrown in to bind it up". Along these tracks he would trudge all the way to Crosthwaite school, but occasionally would get a ride in the Valley's first motor car, driven by Mr. William Wilson of Gutherscale.

It was sometime in that early stage of Eardley's life that a familiar visitor would turn up now and then to discuss the sheep. Beatrix Potter, or as she was by then, Mrs. Heelis, had become a well -respected breeder and judge of Herdwicks. As a young woman at the turn of the century, she had spent many holidays at Lingholm and Fawe Park, just around the hillside on the track from Newlands to Portinscale. Then it was that she had met Lucy, the little daughter of the Newlands Vicar, Benjamin Lund Carr, and the seeds of her story "The Tale of Mrs. Tiggywinkle"were sown. Still one of Beatrix Potter's most popular stories, we read of the hill above Littletown, that went "up, up into the clouds as though it had no top". Many years later, when Beatrix Heelis was living at Sawrey, she had become an expert on sheep diseases, was in great demand as a Show Judge, and in 1930 won the Silver Challenge Cup for the best Herdwick ewe in the Lake District. Her comments and advice were always welcome at Littletown.

Along with others whose families have farmed in the valley for several generations, the Relphs now recall the arrival of cars and petrol driven tractors in the valley, in the later 1940s and 50s. At Littletown the flocks of sheep are roughly the same in number as eighty years ago, but the predominance of the traditional Herdwick has gone, and Swaledales mix with others on the fellsides.

Just past Littletown Farm, snuggling up against the hill, is "Fell Cottage", the plain little stone building which was for so many years the "school-house", and home to Mrs. Jane Foster as she struggled to keep the school up to standard. Eardley Swainson and his wife lived there when it was not required for the schoolmistress. At the time of the 1964 articles in the "Cumbria"magazine, the little school down the hill at the church, was running into real difficulties. Following on from the severely critical Inspectors' reports in the days of Jane Foster, the school had been threatened with closure on several occasions. When this was suggested in 1949, there was strong opposition from the managers and the valley folk. (Many of them had earlier been involved in "up-grading"the school building when it was legally required to offer proper toilet facilities. Farmers, labourers and children alike had helped to dig the trenches for the water pipes!) It was felt that scrapping the school would help the decline in the rural way of life.

During this period, a Miss Dorothea Potts from Portinscale was the mistress in charge. From a Crosthwaite Church magazine, we have the following account of those days, written by her sister Betty. "A few years before the Second World War, a family on holiday was walking through the Newlands Valley when a shower forced them to shelter in the Church."As they looked around, they realised that the little building tacked on to the church was a school. "Little did they know at that moment what a tremendous part that small room was to play in their lives in the years to come.

"Wartime in 1943, and my sister was appointed headmistress of that school. When I returned home at the end of the war, I used to accompany my sister to school every Friday and help with various activities and play the piano for hymn singing, country dancing etc." (How little had changed since the days of Jane Ann Dover!) "Peace time brought more opportunities to travel further, restrictions were lifted, and once again holidaymakers came to stay at the farms in the Valley. One day the County's school dentist came to inspect the childrens' teeth. Teacher asked the class who had cleaned their teeth that morning. Up went everbody's hand except for one small boy whose arm was definitely at half-mast. "Did you clean your teeth or not ?"asked teacher. "Y-yes, oh…y-yes"was the rather flustered reply. "Have you a toothbrush of your own?"suddenly enquired Teacher. "N-naw, not exactly", was the somewhat sheepish reply, "But sometimes Ah use t'visitors'"!

The school outings were varied. The first one in 1946 went to Seascale

Old country ways: Newlands children dancing in the heart of the Valley

and Muncaster Castle grounds. Some children had never seen the sea, as travelling was restricted in the war. In later years there followed visits to ship launchings at Barrow, the Royal Highland Show at Dumfries and many other places of interest. The Open Day and End-of Term Service was the final big event of the school year. Notices of all the events were delivered to every house by the children themselves. "Well, did you get your notices delivered?"asked the teacher on one occasion. "Oh, yes,"came one reply, "and I had my tea at every house!"

Between 1943 and 1962 the number of children attending the school varied between 10 and 26, and their ages ranged at first from 5 to 15 years, then up to 11 years when the secondary modern school opened in 1951. Teaching every subject to such an age range was no easy task, but it was very rewarding to the one who dedicated so much of her life to teaching the children in Newlands School."

At the End of Term Service in the church in August 1962, the Rev. F. H. Marshall spoke of Miss Potts' "wonderful example of faithfulness", of the encouragement she had given the children and the esteem she was held in all over the valley. Presentations of a cheque for £80 and bouquets of flowers to

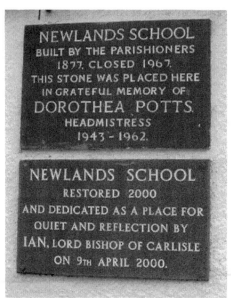

Miss Potts and her sister Betty, were made by Craig and Margaret Beaty, followed by maypole dancing, with Catherine Stillings crowned Queen of the May. Music was provided by Mr. Whitson, one of the managers, and a tea and a display of work in the schoolroom completed the festivities. Among the distinguished visitors were Sir Percy and Lady Hope. A plaque on the wall outside now commemorates the service of Miss Potts to the school.

Commemorative plaque to the teacher, Miss Dorothea Potts, on the wall of the re-furbished schoolroom.

With the retirement of Miss Potts, the dreaded threat of closure loomed again. On April 14th 1962, "The West Cumberland Times" had carried the report that the Western area Authority Committee, by a majority of only one vote, recommended the early closure of Newlands School, despite the petition signed by parents and rate-payers, and forwarded by the school managers. Imagine the indignation of parents and children alike to read in the Times that a Mr. D.G.Wilson, Committee member, had described the Newlands Valley "as only fit for reindeer to live in". There were 16 children at this school when he visited it, and only one toilet. "It was a school which ought to be closed". The decision to close, and send the children to Braithwaite School was only deferred because the latter was also in an unfit state! And so the little band of scholars battled on with their studies, but to Mrs. Isobel Standing fell the sad task of closing the school door for the last time in 1967. The press reported that after the prize giving ceremony, Mrs. Hilda Harryman presented Mrs. Standing with a leather handbag containing a cheque.

For many years the little room was used for various Parish events, scout camps and a variety of meetings, but inevitably, situated out in the Lakeland wind and rain, it fell into a state of disrepair. Many years later, in June 1996, the Keswick Reminder carried a report that the Church Council

An idyllic existence? School teacher Miss Pooley guards her little flock in the 1950s

had decided to restore and refurbish the Schoolroom "in such a way that the essential character of the building is preserved, as a fitting tribute to all that the school has contributed to valley life during the years. Proposals include the re-planning and up-grading of toilet accommodation to provide both standard and disabled facilities", (a far cry from the 1940s "all hands on deck"installations!), a new layout for the kitchen and the provision of modern units, and the complete renovation of the actual schoolroom."With new plumbing, heating and electrical work, the cost was estimated at around £45,000.

Tea-towels, preserves and booklets were sold, letters written to friends all over the world, and Grants received from various sources. The Revd. Campbell Matthews worked tirelessly behind the scenes to pull it all together. Visitors and long-time lovers of Newlands from far-flung places responded magnificently, and now the simply-furnished but cosy room, where teas are served on Sundays during the summer months, is known to many as a place of welcome and peace.

If you visit, do take a moment to sit quietly in the church and remember the history of the valley! Hopefully, the heating will be on if necessary, and you will not have to suffer the cold in the way a previous vicar

Closure! Mrs. Isobel Standing with the last class of pupils at Newlands School, 1967.

did. The Venerable T.R.B. Hodgson, Curate of Crosthwaite in the nineteen fifties, recollects: "The church could be very cold in winter. There was no heating and my wife was sensible enough to bring a hot water bottle and a travelling rug. There were times when I took hot water in a thermos flask for a baptism and filled the family concerned with consternation when they saw the clouds of steam wafting upwards as I prepared the font, before the service, of course. By the time the water was used for pouring onto the baby's head, it was barely tepid."At least the Revd. Hodgson benefitted from the calor gas lighting which was installed in 1953, though electricity did not arrive until many years later!

Inside the church, things have scarcely been changed since the major re-opening in 1885. (The large Royal Coat of Arms, dating from1737, however, must have had an interesting life of its own.) A slate plaque commemorates the refurbishment of 1885, under the auspices of the Rev. H. Whitehead. He had only arrived in Newlands in 1884, and by 1886 disappears from the Registers, but at his very first Vestry meeting, plans were discussed for re-seating and re-flooring the building. Henry Whitehead was not only a man of action, but of compassion and self-sacrifice. Previously Vicar of

Thirty years ago: Mrs. Elizabeth Edmondson clipping a sheep the traditional way at Low Snab Farm.

Brampton, he had been largely responsible for the building of the present church there. But much earlier, during his years as Curate in Soho, London, he had tirelessly pursued his theories on the outbreak of cholera there. In 1854 there were over 500 deaths in Broad Street, Soho. Following up the theory of a Dr. John Snow, that the Broad St. water pump held the key to the outbreak, Henry Whitehead had worked for three months visiting every family affected by the disease. A leaking cesspool was traced, and an important step had been taken in combating and controlling the disease. Although his stay in Newlands was so brief, we hope that the Vicar, in his retiring years, found peace in the beauty of his surroundings.

Only upon close inspection do we find signs of twentieth century life. Standing out brightly among the otherwise unadorned windows, is the memorial glass to soldiers of the Great War. The inscription remembers all in unknown graves, "especially Thomas Roscoe Johnson, who fell in action in France, October 12th 1916, aged 27 years". This window has been something of a mystery to present church-goers, as there has never been any record of Johnsons in the Valley. Investigations have revealed that Thomas, son of John and Honora Johnson of Liverpool, was a private in The King's Liverpool Regiment, aged 27, when he was killed in the fierce fighting near Warlencourt. The faculty for the window was granted to Honora in 1918. The key to the Newlands connection takes us right back to the Holiday Fellowship

Jack Folder at Low House Farm. Forty years after he was featured in Cunbria magazine, Jack still has a few Herdwicks among his sheep on the fells.

Centre at the old woollen mill in Stair, in the days of "Uncle Bill". Among the groups of young men staying there, were several friends from Liverpool. At the outbreak of the War, Lord Derby created the first "Pals Regiment"in Liverpool, and among those enlisting were old friends Frederick Pulford and Thomas Johnson, who had enjoyed walking the fells together on holidays at Stair. They died together, on the same day, in France.

The Roll of Honour hangs on the wall, and several inscriptions around the church tell of benefactors, and sons and daughters of the valley no longer with us.

Twenty one of the schoolchildren in 1937 dedicated a new lectern in memory of the Revd. Richard Bott, and a Bible was given by Betty Mosse. Most recently, a plaque reminds us of the dedication of Mary Clark, organist for over 50 years! Mary was the sister of those two young men who lost their lives in the Air-Force during the war. Today, quiet, reflectional services are held two or three times a month, with a special time of peaceful meditation on Good Friday, when often the worship concludes outside amongst the old tombstones, amongst the yellow splash of the daffodils, and with the bleating of the nearby lambs adding to our praises.

The old and the new at Keskadale Farm.

Leaving the shelter of the church, we walk on up the slopes under Looking Crag, to Low Snab Farm. Here, traditional and more modern ways of farming continue with the Edmondson family. Mrs. Elizabeth Edmondson has kept notes in a diary since the 1930s! Arrivals and departures are faithfully recorded, not only of people but of livestock, cars, tractors, and telephone! She remembers going to the sales with her father in 1954 to buy the first petrol driven tractor in the valley. It still lives at the farm, but is a youngster compared with an old cupboard indoors that dates back to 1643. Three hundred years after the initials of Frank Fischer and Isobella Thwaite were carved on to that cupboard, electricity came to Newlands. Candles and Tilly lamps had provided the lighting until a generator was installed in 1949, with electricity finally reaching Low Snab in 1964. A 1976 edition of "Cumbria"featured Elizabeth clipping sheep at Low Snab, expertly manipulating the shears to relieve the "yow"of her burdensome coat. Mrs. Edmondson is still well known to hundreds of mountain walkers who, over the years, have stopped off at the very tempting sight of her notice, "Pots of Tea", at the end of a long day's tramp. She remembers her mother serving tea to passing "gentry"for 6d, and now continues the tradition as it brings her some welcome company in her very remote farmhouse.

Hidden in a clump of trees below Low Snab is another farm dating way back beyond those earliest manorial records. "Low House"has been the home, at one time or another, to those families of Thwaites, Fishers and Dovers who continued their family lines throughout the sixteenth to twentieth centuries. John (Jack) Folder had his photograph in the Cumbria Magazine in 1964 along with the other valley folk. In those days he and his brother Reuben had a flock of about 1,000 Herdwick ewes ranging the fells over Hindscarth and Dalehead. Even now, at the beginning of the twenty-first century, Low House Farm is the base for the Folders' flock of Herdwicks and Swaledales.

High on the hillside, its creamy "wash"making it very conspicuous against the green fields, stands High Snab Farm. The rough track that goes past it, en route to the lumpy bulk of the mountain curiously named "Robinson", continues uphill past the front of Low High Snab, a very old farm still retaining the simple characteristics of the old 18th century buildings. High Snab itself is now the property of The National Trust. The story of this farm and of the Fishers, Dovers and Cowpers who lived there for so long, eventually concludes with the sale to the Trust in 1969. This, hopefully, has ensured the preservation of the farmhouse and the peace and simplicity of the surrounding area. The trust is the biggest land-owner in the Lake District National Park, but High Snab is its only property in the Newlands Valley. It was bought with the Walmsley-Carter Bequest, and improvements were carried out with a further gift from a regular benefactor, Miss Vaisey. Now, those lucky few who rent the farm for holidays are privileged to be spending their time in one of the most beautiful corners of Cumbria!

On the fellside beyond High Snab, the narrow road winds its way over the Hause towards Buttermere. Nowadays in summer, as everywhere in the Lakes, steady streams of cars make their way along the unfenced, unhedged road. The very last farm they pass is Keskadale, so far from "civilisation"that for generations tourists have wondered what it must be like to live there in winter! The present owners, the Harrymans, have memories stretching way back to the 1920s, many of them carefully preserved in Hilda Harryman's Scrap Book. On the rough road below the farm, coach-and-horse parties would experience the challenge of the "Devil's Elbow", a bend that still challenges car drivers today. Tarmac took over around 1930, and the Harrymans acquired their first car in 1943. With petrol rationing during the war, however, many journeys were undertaken on bicycles or by pony-and-trap. The Harrymans also recollect the digging of trenches in the 1940s to bring mains water to the farms, and the Irish workforce that was brought in to dig in the electricity cables in 1964. The Co-op van used to arrive with the groceries, the fox population was controlled by the huntsmen and hounds, the geese wandered freely, and on high days and holidays the schoolchildren danced around the maypole. Memories of a lost era!

Turning back towards Keswick, we pass above Akin, always one of the smallest farms, which has been developed and is now privately owned, as is the strangely-named "Bawd Hall". Although it is tempting to imagine promiscuous goings-on in the nineteenth century, the historical facts behind the name are no less intriguing. From early in the fifteen hundreds we have records of the Dicconson/Dickinson family as Customary tenants of "Bode Hole". Over the years, scribes struggled to reproduce this name in Parish registers, offering "Boodhol", Boadholle", and even "Boodhoose". Several suggestions have been made as to the origins of the name "Bode Hole", linking it to becks, holes in the wall and even mischievous spirits. Perhaps the rumours of "boggles"and ghosts was one reason why sometimes the house stood empty, frequently in a sorry state. A succession of families held short tenancies until the arrival of Isaac Gill in the mid-1800s, but in 1881, and again in 1901, the house was unoccupied. Sadly, by 1965, only rows of old stones gave a hint of the original lay-out, and the house was completely re-built.

Also tucked well into the hillside below the road, is Gillbrow, where large boulders, remnants of old walls and ancient barns speak of its history. Here, the Wilsons continue traditional farming, and inside the house ancient beams and low ceilings still evoke days gone by.

We are now well on the way to Birkrigg, set high above the road, a fine example of the gradual development of a Newlands farm building during the "Great Re-build". Just before the main farmhouse, is the tiny dilapidated old cottage, which would have been the original Birkrigg farm, and later became the home of "Uncle Peter"and his wife. On one side the almost vertical steps lead down into the old living area, with its huge old fireplace, beams and hooks, and ancient stone floor. On the road level, is the "front door"which until recently sported a large heavy knocker. Hopefully, the present modernisation of the cottage will retain some of its old character.

At the turn of the century, the farmer-cum-church-warden-cum-school-manager John Wilson bought the present Birkrigg farm, and was responsible for extensive renovations, with stables turned into living accommodation, and carefully landscaped gardens. The Beatys who live there now have their own memories of schooldays and wartime. When petrol was short, most of the holiday visitors explored the valley on foot, and Mrs. Beaty senior started selling teas to weary hikers on their way back to Keswick. Bringing this

William Hodgson outside the Swinside Inn, early 1900s.

service to an end was no easy matter, as years after the signs were taken down, people would still be knocking on the farmhouse door hoping for refreshment. Mr. and Mrs. Beaty took a practical interest in the struggling school, as in January 1962, when the intense two-week freeze resulted in the water-system being frozen, and Mr. Beaty, one of the managers, kindly helping out by taking water down in milk-churns. The following year, on the occasion of the marriage, of Princess Alexandra, the school was invited to Birkrigg to watch it on T.V.

At the junction of the road from Littletown stands the eye-catching but sadly derelict "Purple House". Recently known as "Rigg Beck", it was the old Newlands Hotel. In chapter 12, we left the newly-built hotel in the hands of George Bird. Under the management of various families during the first half of the next century, it was the venue for many vale celebrations, wedding receptions, anniversary meals and post-funeral teas. But some years after the war, the larger properties in Newlands became hard to sell and in the 1950s both the old Vicarage and the Newlands Hotel were empty. Privately owned since then, Rigg Beck became a landmark with its coat of purple paint! As this chapter is being written, in 2006, the house is surrounded by scaffolding and shored up by wooden boards. Time will reveal whether this will be lovingly restored for private use, or will become yet another holiday property.

Ignoring the lane that winds back down to the church, we head towards Stoneycroft, passing high above Rowling End Farm. In chapter 12 we saw how the name of the farm and the neighbouring house had gradually evolved over a period of years. In the second half of the twentieth century, the Clarks sold the farmhouse to an eminent Professor of Zoology, Dr. Brierly, and his wife, a renowned Psychoanalyst. The old house, with several alterations and additions, became the venue for many learned and intellectual visitors. Some time later the cottage as well passed into the hands of the family of the present owners.

Not far away, Emerald Bank also witnessed a succession of owners and events, from the war years, with the Misses Frost organising the whist drives, through a period as a guest house, to the present family ownership. Ellas Grag, taking its name from the rocks above, but built on land known as "Ellers" centuries ago, is a twentieth century addition to the valley. Built for Jack Robinson and his wife Annie after the War, it was then home to the Bulman family, with John A. Bulman serving there as National Park Northern Area Manager. And, with a young family there now, is one of the few places in Newlands where children are growing up under the shade of the ancient mountains.

The present Stoneycroft, is built on the site of the old hillside farms mentioned in Court Rolls and Mining transactions. Of all the farms in the valley, perhaps Stoneycroft has the most colourful history, from the days of the 15th century Maysons, the 16th century German Puffparkers, through the Pocklington connections, the later mining activities, and eventually the twentieth century "diversification". During the last hundred years families at Stoneycroft including the Folders, the Wilsons from Watendlath, and the Edmonsons, have continued the farming traditions whilst adding to the range of activities there. On the slopes below the house, it is still possible at the time of writing, to see the scattered and derelict remains of concrete and corrugated-iron sheds. Here, the Edmondsons once had a pig-farm. Mr. Jo Edmondson, who now lives down below the hillside road, at Uzzicar, tells us that at one time there were two and a half thousand pigs on the farm! Unimaginable, but perhaps not such a new idea: amazingly, there is a surviving "Petition" dated 1818, to the Lord of the Manor, in which the lease-holder of Stoney Croft requests timber to repair his "Cart house and Piggary"! In the 1960s, Mr. R. A. Whitson moved into Stoneycroft and ran it as a poultry farm. Eventually all livestock activities at Stoneycroft ceased, and today it is reborn as a private dwelling, with the owners putting a great deal of effort into enhancing their part of the plot. The hotch-potch of sheds and pig-styes below, now called "Ravens Creek", also shows signs of a new lease of life, at the hands of artist and sculptor Peter Nelson, who has embarked upon what should be a most interesting project, including the creation of an artist's studio.

Down below Barrow, all around the Uzzicar area, there is much evidence of the old mining activities. As recently as 1988, an excavation was carried out by the Lakeland Mines and Quarries Trust, to re-discover the site of the 60ft. Water-Wheel, which had been demolished by the start of the first war. High above, the unsightly, scarred slopes of Barrow remind us of the link which our hidden valley has had with the world of industry for many hundreds of years.

Catching the afternoon sunshine high on the Eastern hillside above Uzzicar, are Swinside farm and The Swinside Inn. Originally just the last in a row of tiny cottages, as we can see in the photograph of one W. Hodgson, standing proudly in the doorway early in the twentieth century, the popularity of the establishment grew and grew as the tourist trade increased. An ancient oak cupboard still stands in the oldest part of the pub, underneath the heavy ceiling beams, but it is impossible to identify the old cottage rooms, now serving as kitchens and restaurants for this busy hostelry. Back in the 1970s this change in character was noted by David Imrie, (the gamekeeper and writer behind the name "Oganach"in the wartime newsletter.) On this occasion, the ladies of the W.I produced a booklet about the area, and David was thanked for his help and contributions. Here, we will bring him into Newlands again, at the Swinside Inn, with his poem entitled "Swinside Jerry":

> When first I saw that ancient inn
> Where local dalesmen rally,
> I thought it was the quaintest place
> In lovely Newlands Valley;
> The walls were bulging in and out,
> The roof was sagging badly,
> But no-one spent an evening there
> And tottered homeward sadly!
>
> Old Richard seated by the fire
> Retailed some dialect story,
> And Walt cut in with caustic wit,
> (Though now he's gone to glory).
> And sometimes Willy joined the throng
> To sing a hunting ditty

That made the rafters rattle; for
His topmost notes were gritty.

The inn has changed a lot since then,
  Beyond all recognition;
It caters for a wider class
And seems to have ambition;
But still the worthies gather there
To make an evening merry,
And all the locals as of yore
Yet call it Swinside Jerry.

Our journey from Viking days to twenty-first century is almost complete. We turn our backs on Braithwaite and the Swinside Inn to go down again into Stair. High above us to the East, the cluster of buildings at High and Low Skelgill Farm are home to both visitors and local farmers. The newer house is crushed up against the fellside, hidden by rocks and trees, whilst down the stony slope the rough boulders and dry-stone walls of Low Skelgill still take us back hundreds of years. One happy young holiday-maker at Skelgill in the 1900s was the poet Stephen Spender. He wrote in his autobiography: "The seed of poetry was planted in me when I was nine years old. My parents took us on holiday to Skelgill Farm, near Derwentwater. . . . I remember the rainy lakeside days, and how, after the rain, great raindrops would cling on to the serrated leaves of brambles like hundreds of minute lenses, through which the sun, emerging in a ringed sky, would gleam with a new-seeming whiteness. I remember the long black slugs on paths wrinkled by many torrential downpours, and the smell of the earth, and how on our walks we found rock crystals on the stones like lost enjewelled caskets."

At Skelgill, the late 1900s saw a new twist in the recreational use of old farm buildings. Above the old hay-barn and byre is the Camping Barn, where scores of young fell-walkers have returned, soggy but invigorated, from a day on the summits, to spend the night in basic but economical accommodation.

And so we arrive back in Stair. The Newlands Adventure Centre now occupies the old woollen mill / Holiday Fellowship Centre. Some time after our last look at the Centre's activities, in the 1960s, it was designated as a "base" specifically for Youth Camps. In the "Keswick Reminder" of April 1967 we read of a Mr. Green, a schoolmaster from Preston, who had brought some of his pupils for a holiday. Addressing the local W.I. he showed a film of his children being welcomed to the "Newlands Guest House"by Mr. and Mrs. Bowles, who were to run it for several years. The newspaper reported that the residents were impressed by the schoolchildren's behaviour and politeness, shutting gates and "keeping quiet"(!) "What a wonderful memory in later years this trip must be to the children". Perhaps some of those well-behaved youngsters introduced their own children to the beauty of the Lake District in later years.

Eventually, in 1989, the building was bought by an enthusiastic young team who set up "The Newlands Adventure Centre". A couple of years later the peace of the dale was temporarily disrupted by the camera crew and cast of the childrens' television drama, "Wilderness Edge", filmed entirely in Newlands. The year 2005 saw a landmark at the Adventure Centre, when 100 years of Outdoor Activites were celebrated in grand style, with an exhibition of photographs and historical events and sporting activities. As we look at the activities on offer to young people of the twenty-first century, we wonder what the old mill families and farmers of Newlands would have made of abseiling, kayaking, orienteering, and canoeing!

A final tale of "the old and the new"from the heart of the Vale: in 2006, the ancient packhorse bridge by the church, so often repaired after floods, has suffered extreme damage from that so very modern enemy, heavy traffic. A letter and photograph in The Keswick Reminder has drawn attention to its plight. Our minds go back to that petition of 1734, when a stone bridge "happened lately to fall"and William Dover et. al. pleaded for oakwood for rebuilding!

Our story is complete? No, far from it. With every month that passes, the Vale of Newlands has something new to offer. Be it in changing farm-methods, new property ownership, innovative recreational activities or even Nature's own dramas of flood and storm, one can never predict exactly what life here has in store. Our distant ancestors would have been amazed, shocked and sometimes horrified at what we have done to their land over the centuries. But, to the credit of many farmers, lovers of the Valley and sympathetic developers, we can go on hoping that the spirit of independence and pride in this little paradise will not be lost in years to come.

The Story of the Newlands Valley: Bibliography.

Appleby Andrew, "Famine in Tudor and Stuart England" 1978. Liverpool University.
Bailey J., and Culley G., "A General View of the Agriculture of Cumberland" 1794. London.
Barnes Henry, "Visitations of the Plague", CWAAS, os, Vol. XI.
Bott George, "Keswick, the Story of a Lake District Town". 1994. Cumbria Co. Library.
Bouch C.M.L., and Jones, G.P., "The Lake Counties, 1500-1830." Manchester.
Brunskill R.W., "Vernacular Architecture." London.
Budworth J., "A Fortnight's Ramble to the Lakes". 1795. 3rd. edition 1810.
Clarke J., "A Survey of the Lakes of Cumberland, Westmorland and Lancashire" 1787. London.
Collingwood W.G., "Thirteenth Century Keswick". CWAAS Transactions
"Elizabethan Keswick. Accounts of the German Miners". 1912. Kendal.
Gates Daniel, "The New Shepherds' Guide, 1879.
Grainger Francis, "Agriculture in Cumberland in Ancient Times". CWAAS ns. Vol. IX "The Cumberland Yeoman in Past Times" CWAAS ns. Vol. XIV.
Housman John, "A Topographical Description of Cumberland, Westmorland and Lancashire" 1800, Francis Jollie, Carlisle.
Hutchinson William, "History of the County of Cumberland". 1797.
Lefebure Molly, "Cumberland Heritage." 1970. Golancz.
Marshall J.D., "Old Lakeland". 1971. David and Charles. Newton Abbot.
Martineau Harriet, "A Year at Ambleside", quoted by Barbara Todd in "Harriet Martineau at Ambleside", 2002, Bookcase, Carlisle.
Nicolson and Burn: "History   and   Antiquities   of   Cumberland   and Westmorland". 1777.
Postlethwaite J., "Mines and Mining in the Lake District". 1913. Whitehaven.
Rawnsley H.D., "Life and Nature at the English Lakes" 1902. Glasgow.
"By Fell and Dale at the English Lakes." 1911. Glasgow. "Literary Associations of the English Lakes". 1901. Glasgow.
Rollinson W., "Life and Tradition in the English Lake District". 1974. London. "A History of Man in the Lake District". 1967. London.
Taylor Jeff, "Our Lizzie".
Walpole Hugh, "Rogue Herries". 1936. Macmillan. London.
West Father Thomas, "Guide to the Lakes". 1812. 2nd edition. Pennington. Kendal.
Wilberforce William, "Journey to the Lake District from Cambridge". 1779. Oriel Press.
Wilson Tom, "The History and Chronicles of Crosthwaite Old School". 1949. McCane, Keswick.
Winchester Dr. Angus, "Landscape and Society in Medieval Cumbria", Edinburgh, John Donald, 1987. "The Harvest of the Hills", Edinburgh University, 2000.
Wordsworth W., "Guide to the Lakes". Selincourt, 5th edition, 1835. Kendal.

Acknowledgements

Many of the original 17th and 18th century documents which have given such insights into earlier life in the Valley, have been made accessible from the archives at Cockermouth Castle, by kind permission of Lord Egremont. My thanks also go to the staff at both Carlisle and Whitehaven Record Offices, and at Keswick Library, for their help in my stumbling first steps in research. I am indebted, too, to Bill Thwaite for the precious "Bull" notebook, to Peter Williams for the Newlands Church Wardens Accounts and the Above Derwent Newsletter, to the Newlands Adventure Centre for access to Uncle Bill's Diary, and to Carole Handy for The Gates' Shepherds Guide.

The Revds. Reg. Harper, Campbell Matthews and Burnham Hodgson all shared thoughts and material with me, and my thanks go too to the many people who have written from a distance to tell me of their family connections with Newlands.

My thanks to those who have supplied photographs: Jeff Taylor, Rob Grange, Dr. W. M. Mitchell and Hilda Harryman.

Above all, I have enjoyed getting to know those who live in the old farms now. Listening to their reminiscences of family characters and legends helped to bring the whole scene to life.

Finally, Colin, my IT consultant, my patient husband who rescued me so often from black holes on the computer screen. Without him I'd still be on chapter 3!

Books Published by Bookcase

Keswick Characters: Volume One £7.99

The first volume of a series by members of the Keswick Museum telling the life stories of the many eminent and interesting people who have llived in Keswick over the years. This volume includes Sir John Bankes, Jonathan Otley, Joseph Richardson & Sons, Henry Cowper Marshall, John Richardson, George Smith - the Skiddaw Hermit, James Clifton Ward, Hardwicke Drummond Rawnsley, Tom Wilson and Ray McHaffie

The Loving Eye and Skilful Hand: The Keswick School of Industrial Arts. Ian Bruce. £15.00

This is the first detailed study of the Keswick School. Founded by the Rawnsleys, the school became one of the most important centres of the Arts and Crafts movement. The book should be of great interest to historians and collectors..

Keswick: The Story of a Lake District Town. George Bott. £15

This elegant history tells the story of Keswick from the time of Castlerigg Stone Circle to the present day. Keswick has an importance far beyond its size. German miners came in Elizabethan times, the pencil was discovered here, it was a key centre of the Romantic revolution and later the town became famous for the Keswick Convention.

The Wigton Memorial Fountain   Solway History Society   £10

In 2004 Solway History Society restored the George Moore Memorial Fountain which stands in the centre of Wigton. This book tells the story of the fountain and of George Moore who built it as a memorial to his wife, Eliza. There is a detailed photographic record of the Fountain itself and a pictorial record of the Fountain through the years.

A Canny History of Carlisle. Jim Eldridge. £7.99

Caught on the cusp between England and Scotland, Carlisle has a better story to tell than most cities. Our Canny Historian, Jim Eldridge,creator of Radio 4's King Street Junior, is just the chap to tell the tale of the Great Border City - from the days of the Celts and the Romans right up to the floods and the football team.

Carlisle to Canada: A Family Chronicle. Cathy Smith   £8.99

Cathy Smith discovered a bundle of old letters in her grandmother's house in Melbourne Road, Carlisle. They told of an Edwardian romance and of emigaration to Canada and the parallel lives two families led in Carlisle and on a prairie farm.